Master the Art of Unreal Engine 4 - Blueprints

A selection of Blueprint projects crafted with the goal of helping you become a master of Unreal Engine 4's Blueprints system

Master the Art of Unreal Engine 4 - Blueprints

First Published: 28/09/2014

Production Reference: 014180MM0-2

ISBN-13: 978-1501054297
ISBN-10: 1501054295

www.kitatusstudios.co.uk
Cover image by Ryan Shah (contact@kitatusstudios.co.uk)

Credits

Author

    Ryan Shah

Special Thanks

    Scarlett Juzzle
- Thank-You Scarlett for putting up with me, I have so much love for you it's UNREAL.

    Scott Heyworth
- Thank-You for being a great pal and also all of the music for Kitatus Studios!

    Matt Toyer
- Thank-You for being my best buddy throughout the years.

    Hourences
- Thank-You for inspiring me to help others!

    xTomass
- Thank-You for supporting me, doing the interviews and providing voice Work for Kitatus Studios!

    WeiseGamer
- Thank-You for the coverage and being a great guy!

    Daniel Dunham
- Thank-You for being the first to support Kitatus Studios!

    John Romero
- Thank-You for taking the time out to give me some pointers for Super Distro and for the kind words!

    Epic Games
- Thank-You for making such an awesome tool that has revolutionized Game development!

    Square Enix Montreal
- Thank-You for the morale boost and kind words about Super Distro!

About the Author

Ryan Shah is Project Lead / Lead Developer at Kitatus Studios. Boasting over 10 years of experience creating video-games, Ryan has worked on an assortment of different programs to create video-game experiences.

Before Kitatus Studios, Ryan was a freelance writer, who self-published works of fiction. Using his experience as a writer, Ryan turned to video-games, a lifelong passion to bring the worlds of his ideas to life.

He can be found online at http://kitatusstudios.co.uk and can be contacted at contact@kitatusstudios.co.uk

Acknowledgement

A huge thank-you and a half has to go to my beautiful girlfriend Scarlett, who no matter what has always believed in me when nobody else did. Her patience is inspiring.

I'd like Epic for creating such a diverse yet easy to use system with Unreal Engine 4. When people say it's a game changer, they weren't wrong!

I'd also like to thank my parents; Because without them, you wouldn't be reading this right no! I'm also throwing a shout-out to my brothers, Kallum and Jordan. I hope this book inspires them to follow the career path I chose and they see just how fun it can be to create video-games! I'd also like to thank you, the reader. I might not know you personally, but by you buying this book - You're helping to support me and helping to support the video-game industry. Who knows - Maybe this book will help you and become the stepping stone you need to make the BEST GAME OF ALL TIME. Anything is possible!

Preface

Unreal Engine 4 is the latest version of the popular video-game development package; the Unreal Engine. The Unreal Engine needs no introduction; Being the powerhouse behind the previous console generation from the start. To call the Unreal Engine a powerhouse would be an understatement, the Unreal Engine is everything a developer (Indie and Commercial) would ever need in a video-game engine to create their ideal project. With it's latest iteration, Unreal Engine 4, Epic has improved Unreal Engine and propelled the engine into the next-generation, they have brought the future to the present with Unreal Engine 4 and there's literally never been a better time to begin using Unreal Engine 4 for any project, big or small, commercial or independent.

Mastering the Art of Unreal Engine 4 - Blueprints takes a concise, clear, informative but fun approach to developing Unreal Engine 4, without touching a single line of code. By using this book, you'll be creating various small projects completely in blueprint. From this book, you'll be equipped with the know-how you'll need to create the game of your dreams. On top of mastering the Blueprints system in Unreal Engine 4, you'll also learn the secrets behind getting the most out of the beast of an engine.

What this Book Covers

Here's what you'll learn thanks to this book *without writing a single line of code!*
- How to create animated textures with Flipbook
- How to create portals to transition between two levels
- How to create a loading screen!
- How to create a HUD!
- What is the difference between a Bool, Int, Float, String and Array?
- How to Kill a Player!
- Switching Players!
- Altering Materials!
- Keeping Score!
… And much, much more!

What You'll Need For This Book

In order to take full advantage of this book; You'll need a Windows, Mac or Linux computer that is capable of running Unreal Engine 4. It requires a computer with the following system configuration, which doubles up at the "Minimum Requirements" for this book:

- Desktop PC or Mac
- Windows 7 64-bit or Mac OS X 10.9.2 or later
- Quad-core Intel or AMD processor, 2.5 GHz or faster
- NVIDIA GeForce 470 GTX or AMD Radeon 6870 HD series card or higher
- 8 GB RAM

Note: Believe it or not, You'll also need Unreal Engine 4 (Version 4.2 or newer).

Who this Book is For

Mastering the Art of Unreal Engine 4 - Blueprints is designed for anyone whose dreamt of creating video-games, but didn't have the knowhow to. This book is also designed for everyone who wants to harness the power of Unreal Engine 4 to take their creations to the next level and beyond and the people who want to create games without writing a single line of code.

Those who are familiar with Unreal Engine 4 will have an easier time, but everything in the book is explained clearly and with reference screenshots to make the process of mastering the blueprints system in Unreal Engine 4 a breeze. People with no prior experience to using Unreal Engine 4, or game engines in general should have no problem with following this book, but if you need additional help with anything in the book, feel free to ask on the Unreal Engine Forums (http://forums.unrealengine.com) or email me directly: contact@kitatusstudios.co.uk.

Reader Feedback

I love feedback! Good or bad, it's all welcome and I highly recommend you do so! If you loved reading or hated it, I seriously would love to know. Feedback is important in helping letting me know how I've done, what needs to be fixed and I'm just generally intrigued on how well / bad I've done. I'm a perfectionist and I strive for the best, so if there's anything I can improve on, feel free to email: contact@kitatusstudios.co.uk

Customer Support

Since you're the owner of this book, You have the opportunity to get bonus content, such as colour images and project content: Head to http://content.Kitatusstudios.co.uk to access to these files!

Piracy

I'm not going to pretend it doesn't exist; Piracy is piracy and nothing is going to stop it. If you've pirated this book; It's alright. I'm not going to curse you... It's sad that you're not willing to spend money on this book, but I know times are tough and in the digital world I know that everything is free to some people.

Due to the fact I've given up the time to write this book to help teach others to harness the power of Blueprints, losing out on work hours and time I could have spent on *Super Distro* (My first Commercially to-be-released project), I ask that if you pirated this book and you've enjoyed this book, Please consider purchasing Super Distro or you could send a donation through my website. This means that even if you don't spend the full-price on this book, My efforts to bring these tutorials to you aren't 100% in vein.

If you've purchased this book, then I can't thank-you enough for supporting me and my work and I seriously am grateful you're experiencing the book through legitimate means.

Errata

At the time of writing, the book has no errors. However, as the engine is updated, things might change. In the unlikely event some of the code no longer works, please email me immediately: contact@kitatusstudios.co.uk - By doing this, you not only secure the integrity of the book, but you also help others by not coming across errors and this leads to a stress-free experience with this book. Who knows, you might also be credited in later book revisions!

Downloading DLC (Downloadable Content)

You can download colour variations of the images in this book, as well as UE4 project files from http://content.kitatusstudios.co.uk.

Questions

If you have any questions, email me at contact@kitatusstudios.co.uk. The line is open, so please don't be afraid to get in touch.

Mission #1 - Now You're Thinking With Portals

An introduction in UE4 and Blueprints.

Template:
Blueprint Third person

What You'll Learn:
- Transition between two levels
- How to create a Loading Screen
- Animated Textures
    (Flipbook Animations)
- Create a Hubworld
    (An area which connects all your levels)

What You'll Need:
- Portal Texture
    - If Animated: You'll Need the Animation
        and GlueIt, which is available here:
http://www.varcade.com/blog/glueit-sprite-sheet-maker-download/
- Loading Screen (.PNG or .TGA)
    - Dimensions: 1920 x 1080

(Extras) What You'll Need for Extras:
- Animated Portal Video (.Mov) / .GIF file

Let's Begin!

First things first, let's fire up Unreal Engine 4 and create a new project!

Open up Unreal Engine 4 and you'll be greeted with this screen:

This is the launcher; Where you'll spend the first few moments every time you open Unreal Engine. I seriously recommend checking out the Marketplace content; Especially the Content Examples. These Marketplace items are a gold-mine of information of how Epic (the Unreal Engine developers) use the engine to put their content together.

Epic have also stated that all the content on the Marketplace is free for re-use (Within Unreal Engine 4 projects) which is an absolute bonus for being able to use their textures, materials, props and models for personal learning.

For most of the content on the Marketplace, there's a documentation page over on the Unreal Wiki (https://docs.unrealengine.com/latest/INT/) - So you'll be able to break apart the content and learn from every little detail, which I can't stress enough is such an invaluable resource for developers just starting out with Unreal Engine 4.

Creating a New Project

Starting right off the bat on the launcher, we'll hit the "Launch" button to begin our Unreal Engine 4 Adventures.

It'll take a moment or two, but once it's loaded, you'll be greeted with this screen:

Please note that your screen might look at little different to mine, as it all depends on what projects you've created / installed.

On the top of this screen, there's a "New Project" tab. Seeing as this example will have us creating some portals in the third person example, we'll go ahead and pick that one, making sure that we're choosing **Blueprint Third Person** NOT Code third Person (You might have to scroll down to find Blueprint Third Person!). ***Also, be sure to name your project on the bottom of the screen and make sure "Include Starter Content" is ticked!***

Once you're ready to begin, press "Create Project" and Unreal Engine 4 will set up our project for the first time (This will take longer than usual as it's setting up project files).

Once the project has been loaded, you'll be greeted with this screen:

This means everything has been set up correctly and we can begin our work on "Project: Let's Make a Friggin' Portal!"

If you want to try the project as it is, on the bar just above the "Play Area", there are a number of options. If you press Play, you'll be thrown into the game. This'll give you the opportunity to run around and get a feel for the engine. So if you haven't already, I highly recommend doing that.

After you've had a little run around, it's time to begin working on our Portal system!

First things first, We'll need a new map to transition to, so let's create a new map now by going to File > New Level...

You're presented an option of "Default or Empty Level" - For this example, Default will do nicely.

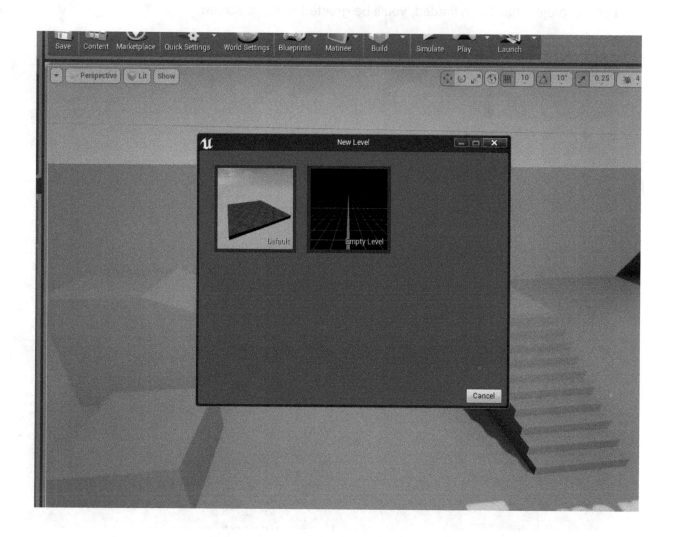

Once the level has loaded, we'll need to save it quickly so we don't lose any data! Head up to File > Save As...

It should open into your Content/Maps folder, if it doesn't it shouldn't be too hard to find. Once you're in the folder, type in your Map name and click "Save".

Remember what you call this level as it'll be VITAL later! I've called mine ArtOf_Example2, but you're free to call yours what you like.

UNREAL ENGINE 4 ETIQUETTE - FILE NAMES - When naming files, The best way of doing it is by a short summary as a prefix, followed by an underscore and the file name. For example: A character blueprint should be called Char_*Charactername* and a map shoud be named PROJECTNAME_MAPNAME (Example: ArtOfBp_Example2). This helps keep your Unreal Engine 4 project clean and concise and make it easy to find anything should you need to locate it.

Now our map has been created, you can go ahead and return to the example map: File > Open Level > Example_Map.

Once back into the map, it's time to mess around with portals! In the content browser, Hit the shiny "New" button and click on Blueprint.

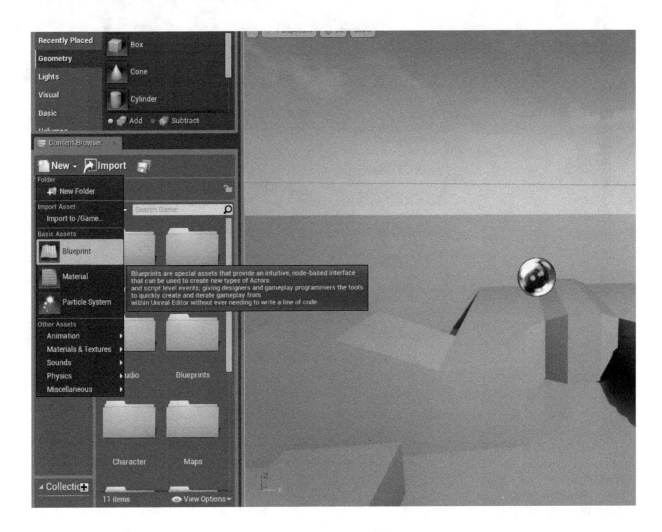

It'll then open up a dialog box asking what kind of Blueprint we want to create. For the portal, we'd like an *Actor blueprint*, so go ahead and click Actor:

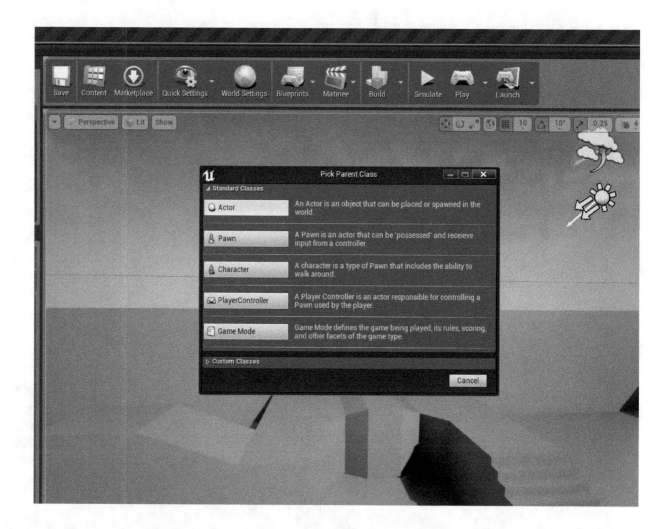

Now comes the time to name our Blueprint, so I'm going to be using "BP_Portal". Again, you're free to use whatever you like as a name. If by chance, you accidently clicked away and would like to rename your Blueprint, simply Right Click (Ctrl+Click on a Mac) and select rename (TIP: You can also left click the Blueprint and press F2).

Once you've altered the name of your Blueprint, Press New on the Content Browser again and press "Folder", this will create a new folder. Name this "TutorialContent".

When you've created your folder, simply click and drag your blueprint into the folder and a small box will appear asking whether you want to "Copy Here" or "Move Here". For our situation, we'd like to move it to the folder, so click "Move Here" and the Blueprint will be transported to it's new location.

Now double click the Folder and you should have a Content Browser that looks like this:

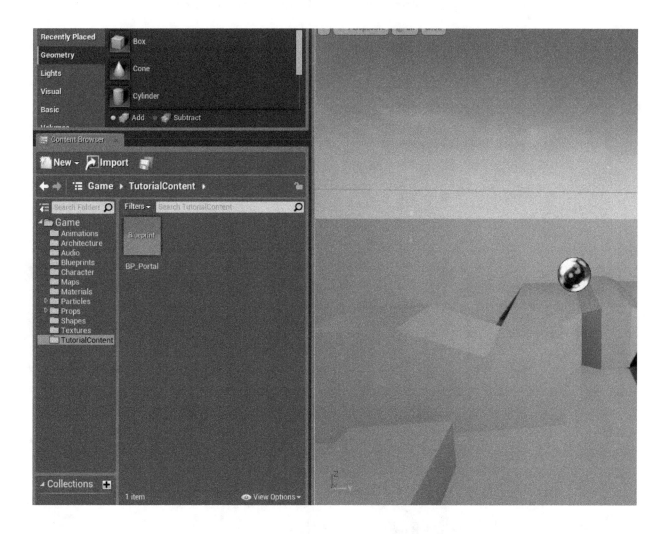

Now is time to import your Texture for the Portal. Here is where we'll branch into two different areas. Even if you're using a non-animated portal texture, please do read through the tutorial behind the Animated Portal Texture, as this will teach you the core ideas behind Flipbooks and animations in Unreal Engine 4:

For Non-Animated Portal Texture:

If the texture you wish to import for your Portal is static (Doesn't move), then all you'll need to do is import the texture and convert it into a material. The way we do this is by going to Import, which is next to the New button in the Content Browser.

Then find your Portal texture and import it. It should import into your TutorialContent folder. If an error comes up saying it's not a "Power of Two" texture, that's fine, just click continue. If it is in a different folder, simply drag and drop it inside the TutorialContent folder.

Once your texture has been imported, Right click the texture and select the option "Create Material…"

This will create a Material; But we still have work to do!

Double-click the created Material to load up the Material editor; This is where we can edit the properties of the Material.

When you first load up the Material Editor, the "Base Colour" node might be inside the main tree of nodes. This is not a problem, just click and drag the Material away from it and you should now be looking at something that looks like this:

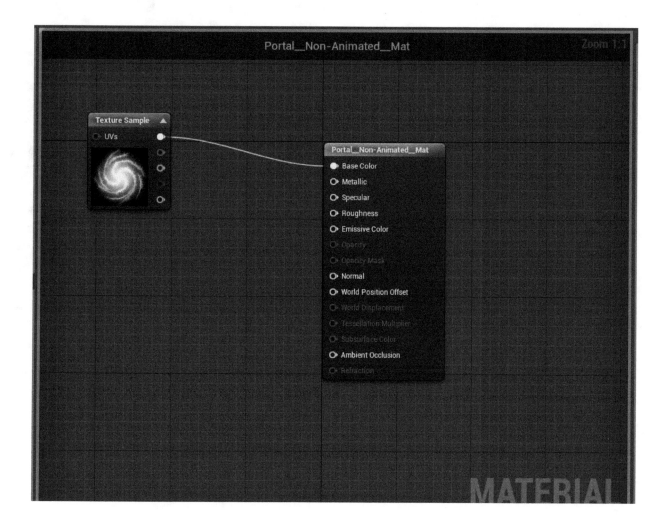

We don't need to do much at the moment, We'll be back for more in later projects. We first need to connect the Texture Sample to the Emissive Color channel in the Material editor.

What is Emissive Color? - To sum up Emissive Color into as short as possible: Emissive Color is the property that sets what colour comes OUT of the material. Think of something you don't want to be affected by any lights around it, such as a Neon sign or a point of interest.

By putting the texture into Base Colour and Emissive Colour, it will make the material glow as if it were a Television / Computer screen or a light source similar to that. If you want to read more into what the material properties are and what they mean, You can find all this information on the Unreal Engine website in the "Official Documentation", which can accessed by pressing F1 in the Unreal Engine.

Anyway, For now, left click where the white output is on "Texture Sample" and drag and drop the line so it sits in Emissive Color. Now Texture Sample should be hooked up to Base Color and Emissive Color, like this:

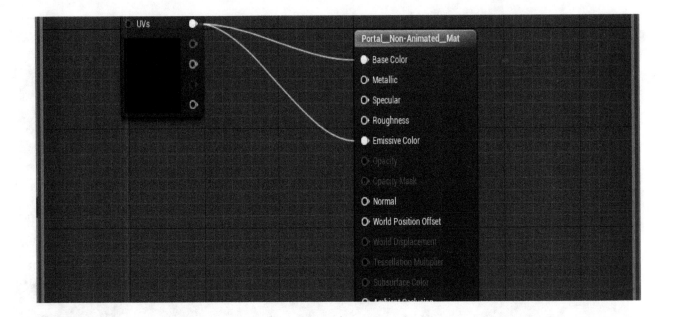

IMPORTANT TIP: Whenever you make a change to a blueprint or Material within Unreal Engine, make sure to Save (Which will automatically "Apply" too, so you don't have to hit both buttons over and over again) which will make sure you don't lose any changes if your editor crashes at any point.

To save, hit that juicy big save button on the top of your Material editor:

Once you've saved, you can close the Material editor. Make sure to also "Save All" in the main Unreal Engine window; This ensures you don't lose any data.

For Animated Portal Texture:

This is where it gets a little tricky. I'll explain this as simply as possible, but if you get lost just re-trace your steps and you should be okay. Are you ready?

If you want your Portal texture to be animated, we're going to need a Flipbook, which is Unreal Engine's answer to 2D animation. To create a Flipbook and for it to work properly, we're going to need a Spritesheet. To do this, we're going to employ the help of "GlueIt" - A free application created by "Vacade" (Link is in the Project Outline at the start of this Chapter) . GlueIt will turn out movies / GIFs into Spritesheets but it can't do it all itself. First, we need to convert our video / GIF into a sequence of images for GlueIt to work its magic.

There are a few ways we can convert our Video / GIF to an image sequence, here are two different ways we can achieve this with two different software packages; QuickTime Pro (Not Free - Video & GIF supported) and VLC Media Player (Free - Video supported, GIF is not supported). (**NOTE: There are other ways of doing this, however if you'd like a guide on alternative ways to convert Video / GIF into an image sequence, I recommend looking on your favourite search engine**).

QuickTime Pro:

Step #1 - Open your Video / GIF File

Step #2 - File > Export

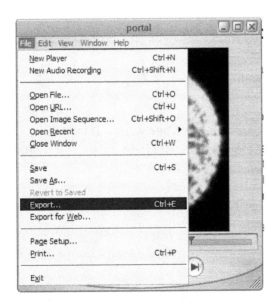

Step #3 - Create a New Folder (**TIP: Remember where it is!**) - Call it something along the lines of PortalAnim (The name isn't too important).

Step #4 - Open the Folder, ready to Export there. Set Export to "Image Sequence" using "BMP, 25 fps".

Step #5 - Export!

VLC Media Player:

Step #1 - Create a New Folder on your PC /Mac /Linux (**TIP: Remember where it is!**) - Call it something along the lines of PortalAnim (The name isn't too important). Make sure to Copy (Ctrl + X / Ctrl + C) the folder's location **<- VERY IMPORTANT**

Step #2 - *DO NOT OPEN* your Video File **YET** (In VLC)

Step #3 - Go to Tools > Preferences

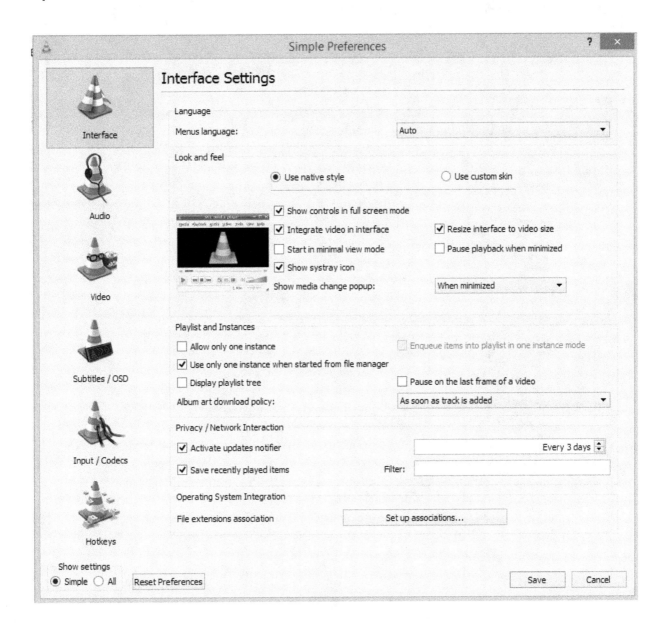

Step #4 - Where it says "Show Settings" at the bottom of the "Simple Preferences" Window, you're given a choice of "Simple" or "All". Set it to All.

Step #5 - You'll now be given a list view of all the settings. Scroll down to Video and select Filters. On the right, select "Scene Video Filter". Once this has been checked, Expand filters on the left and look for "Scene Filter". Click it.

Step #6 - On the right hand side, there is an option that says "Directory Path Prefix". In this box, paste the path to the folder you created in Step #1.

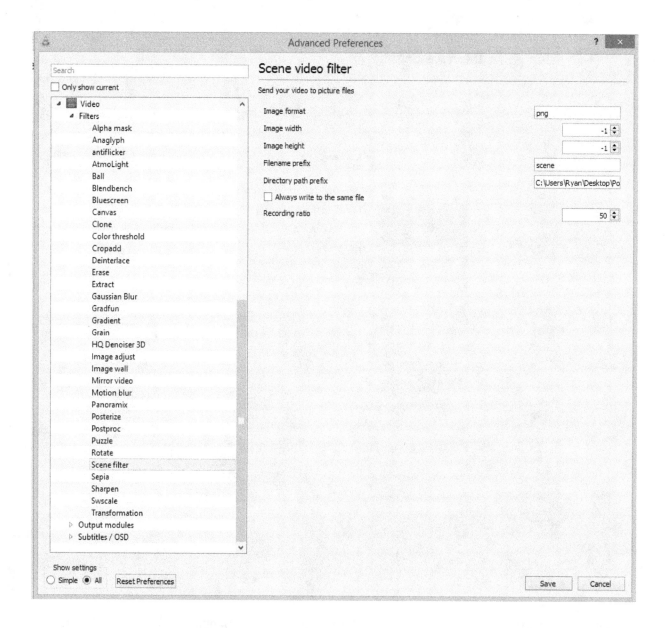

Step #7 - Just underneath "Directory Path Prefix", there is a box called Recording Ratio. This is the amount of frames you'd like to export, for example I have 3 frames and if I put in 50, it would record every 50th frame. 24 should be that limit, in my opinion. Set this accordingly.

Step #8 - Press Save at the bottom when you're done.

Step #9 - Go to File > Open File and open your video.

Step #10 - Let the video play to the end. It should only be a couple seconds long.

Step #11 - After your video has finished playing go back into preferences and back to Video > Filters and deselect "Scene Video Filter" (This stops VLC recording the frames of every video you open.

Now we're ready for the next step…

GlueIt

Once you've downloaded GlueIt, it's time to open the application and begin stitching together our "Image Sequence".

When GlueIt has opened, it's time to import our images. At the bottom of GlueIt, we have three buttons under Step #1: Add, Delete and Clear. We want to Add our images, so go ahead and add them, but **before** you do, we have a branching pathway coming up so it's best to address it here:

Depending on the amount of frames you've got, we have to take something important into account: ***Unreal Engine only supports textures up to 8,192 x 8,192.*** Normally this won't be a problem as your portal texture shouldn't be more than approximately 512 x 512-ish each frame. But if for example you have a 1920 x 1080 movie that spans 40-50 frames, it's not going to fit into Unreal Engine, so you'll need to break the GlueIt's into multiple files so the Unreal Engine will accept the files.

This will take a little tinkering, but sometimes it's best to import "Frame 1 > 10" (For example) into GlueIt and after it's saved, importing "Frame 11 > 20" .etc. Make sure that no matter how many columns you set up, you do this for all the GlueIts in the sequence, this helps keep your Material blueprint clean and easy to manage.

Now we've got that out of the way, it's time to add our images. For the sake of this project, I'm going to be using an Animated portal that would fit nicely on a single spritesheet. But further along in this tutorial, I will be accommodating for if you have multiple spritesheets.

Step #1 - In the Step #1 Section of GlueIt, Add your images (Or selection of Images to that are for this Spritesheet)

Step #2 - Once your Images have been added, move to Step #2 in the GlueIt Window. It's now time to set how many columns we need. In order to make sure there's no white / black boxes at the end of our animation, let's make sure our amount of frames fit perfectly on the sprite sheet.

For example, if I have 20 frames and two columns, there's 10 frames on each column. BUT if we have 3 columns, this would be split amongst three columns; Leaving a lot of empty space at the end of our spritesheet, We don't want this as it'll complicate things later.

As previously stated, as I have 20 frames, two columns would be perfect. Important tip: **REMEMBER how many columns you've used and remember how many rows this will create too, we'll need this later!**

Once you've set the columns, press GlueIT and give it a moment to glue your images together!

Step #3 - Once Glued, Press Save (Make sure you remember where you save it to!)

Now that we have our Spritesheet, we need to get it into Unreal Engine to begin animating our Portal!

Making the Animated Material

So now that we have our Spritesheet, we need to import it into Unreal Engine. Just import it like any normal texture (Like we've done already!) - For a quick refresher to help drill in just how simple that is:

Step #1 - In the Content Browser (The box where all of your files are), at the top of this window, Next to "New" is a button called "Import". Click it.

Step #2 - Find your Spritesheet that GlueIt created and Import; If an error comes up saying it's not a "Power of Two" texture, that's fine, just click continue.

Step #3 - Right click your texture and "Create Material"

Now that the texture is in the engine and turned into a Material, This is where it's going to get a little complicated if you have more than one sprite sheet; But I'll try my best to make the process as simple as possible:

If you have One Sprite Sheet:

Step #1 - Open up the Material Editor by double click your Material.

Step #2 - Inside the Material Editor, Left Click "Texture Sample" (Connected to Base Colour) and press Delete on your keyboard or Right Click (Ctrl + Click) and press Delete. Your Material Editor should now look like this:

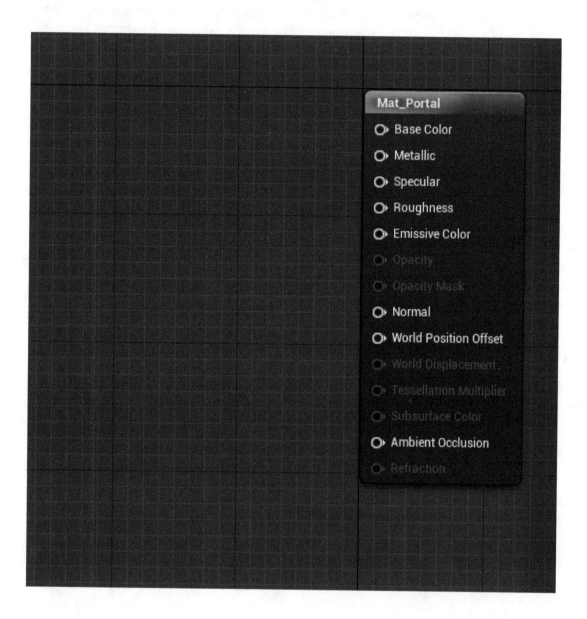

Step #3 - From the "Base Colour" pin, click the pin and drag to the left into empty space. When the prompt box comes up, write in "Flipbook". Click the option that comes up and a Flipbook will be created in your Blueprint, pre-connected into your Base Colour pin.

Step #4 - Where the Flipbook connects to the "Base Colour", Drag the filled in pin and drag over to the "Emissive Colour" Channel. This will create a link to Emissive Colour to the Flipbook, while keeping the link to Base Colour. You should now have a Material that looks like this:

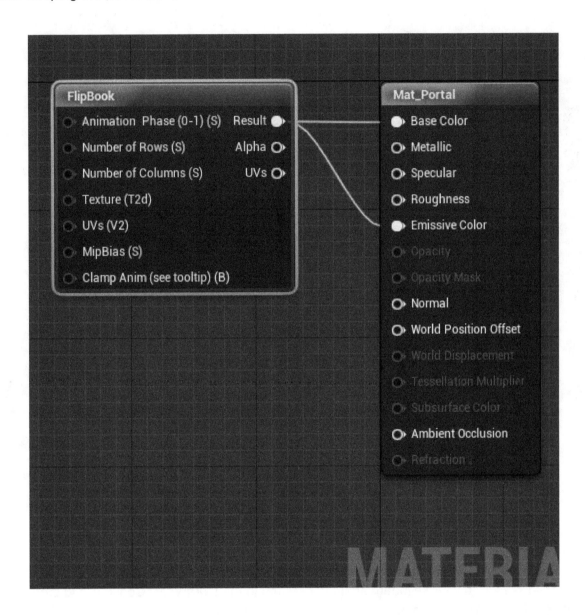

Step #4 - To the left of your Flipbook node, Press the number "1" on your keyboard (The one under your F1, F2, F3 .etc), this will create a "Constant" (Alternatively, you can type "Constant" into the search box above the library on the right and it'll find it for you).

Step #5 - Click the newly created "Constant" and on the left, you'll find the properties. In this properties box, there's a field called: "Value:" with 0.0 already inputted. For our example, type in the number of rows your Flipbook has. For me, the number is 5 (As I have ten images in two columns):

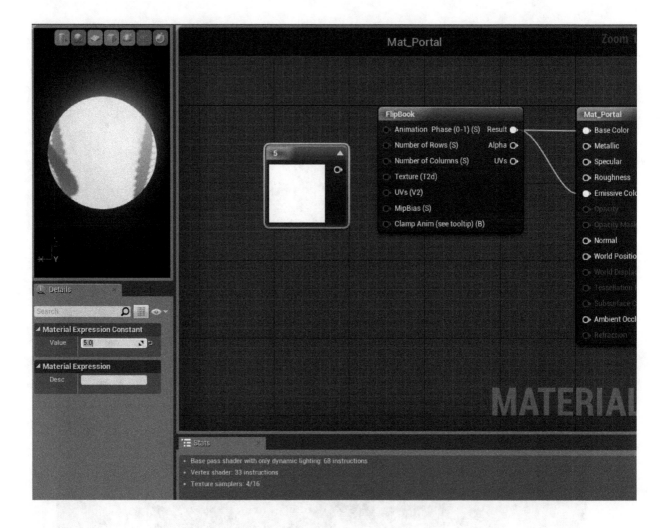

Step #6 - Drag the open pin of your "Constant" to the "Number of Rows" node in your FlipBook.

Step #7 - Press 1 on your keyboard again (Or search in the Library for "Constant") to create another constant. This one is our Column number. For my texture, this is 2 (As I have 20 images split into two columns, 5 rows). Change the value and put in your amount of Columns. Once inputted, drag the open pin of your Constant into the "Number of Columns" of your flipbook.

HELPFUL TIP: On the top right of your Constant nodes, there is a little grey arrow. Pressing this will toggle the colour box to appear and disappear. For the sake of keeping your Blueprints neat and tidy, you can go ahead and toggle the colour up, so we only see the number value.

Step #8 - Your Material should now look a little like this:

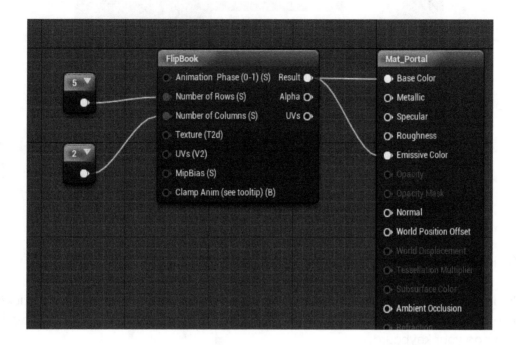

Now, underneath your Constants and the Flipbooks, Right click (Ctrl + Click) and this will bring up a compact version of the Blueprint Library. In the search field at the top type "Texture Object", this will reveal a few options. The one we're looking for is "Texture Object", so click it and it will create a Texture Sample node.

Click your newly created "Texture Object" and on the left in your Properties box, there is a box named "Texture". Just to the right of this box, there is a dark gray box with "None" written in it. Click this box and in the search box that appears type in the name of your Spritesheet. My Spritesheets name is "TEX_PortalAnim" so I'll type that in and select it. This will set the "Texture Object" node to become the "Spokesperson" so-to-speak for our Texture:

Step #8 - Hook up your Texture Object's white pin to the "Texture(T2d)" node of your Flipbook.

Step #9 - In the "UVs" pin of your Flipbook, Click the pin and drag to the left. This will load up the "Compact Blueprint" library again. In the search box, this time type: "TextureCoordinate" and Press Enter on your keyboard.

This will create a TextureCoordinate, which the Unreal Engine documentation describes as: "*The TextureCoordinate expression outputs UV texture coordinates in the form of a two-channel vector value allowing materials to use different UV channels, specify tiling, and otherwise operate on the UVs of a mesh.*"

Step #10 - Remember to Save by pressing the floppy disc widget at the top of the Material Editor! You can now exit the Material editor.

If you have More than One Spritesheet:

This is not advised for beginners. We're going to be stepping into some pretty complicated territory.

To get a glimpse on how complicated this step can get:

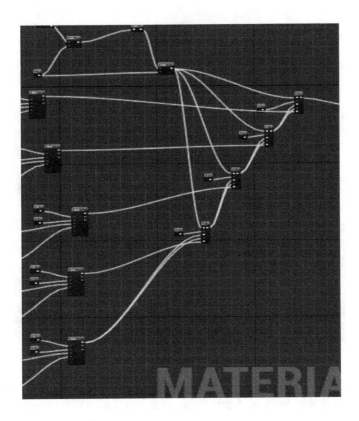

Step #1 - Open up the Material Editor by double click your Material.

Step #2 - Inside the Material Editor, Left Click "Texture Sample" (Connected to Base Colour) and press Delete on your keyboard or Right Click (Ctrl + Click) and press Delete.

Step #3 - From the "Base Colour" pin, click the pin and drag to the left into empty space. When the prompt box comes up, write in "If". Click the option "If" that comes up and an "If" node will be created in your Blueprint, pre-connected into your Base Colour pin.

Step #4 - On the If Node, Pins "A", "A>=B" and "A<B" all NEED to be filled in for the Blueprint to compile. So in order to make our Blueprint work, we're going to use a time system; So our Material knows which Spritesheet to play at any given time.

From Pin "A" of the "If" node, Drag to the left and the Compact Blueprint Library loads up once more. From this, select "Multiply".

We need a Multiply node as we're going to be going be taking the decimal number of "Time" (After it's been divided) and multiplying it with a number (In our case, I urge you mess around with the number we're going to create as it'll let you alter the speed of your Flipbooks).

Your Material should now look like this:

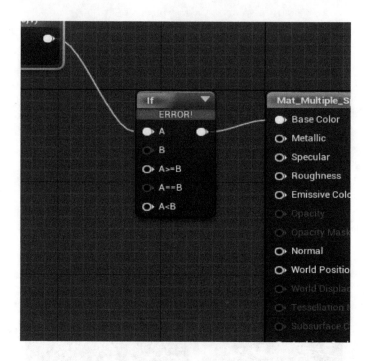

Step #5 - From the A pin of our "Multiply" node, Drag to the left again and in the search box, type in "Frac", this will get the decimal from Time and multiply it with a number to define the speed of our Flipbooks.

Step #6 - From the empty left side pin of "Frac" drag to the left and in Compact Blueprint Library, type in "Divide" and press enter. This will give us a Divide node, which we'll need to divide the time with our number we set for the speed of our Flipbook animation.

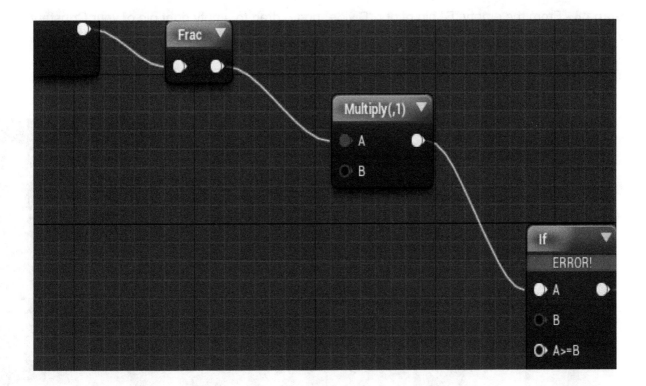

Step #7 - From the empty "A" pin of our "Divide", drag to the left and in the search box that appears, type in "Time" and select the Constant "Time" that appears, this is our key "Time" component that this whole Material relies on.

Step #8 - Below our "Time" node, Press 1 on your Keyboard (Or search in the Blueprint library for Constant) to create a Constant. In the properties (In the lower left of your screen) set the value of the Constant to 5.

This is the speed of your Material's animation and might need to be changed later.

Step #8 - From the empty "B" pin of our "Divide" node, drag to empty right pin of your Constant to connect them together.

Your blueprint should now look a little like this:

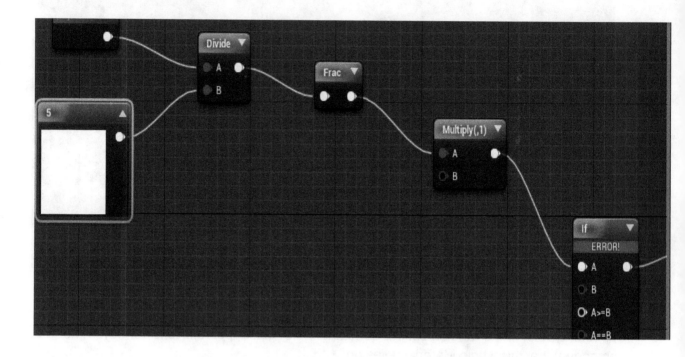

Step #9 - From the filled in White pin of our Constant (Which is already connected to "Divide"), click and drag to the B of Multiply, which should currently be empty. This will establish a link from the Constant to not only Divide but to Multiply.

Currently, this means that the Material is currently:
Checking the time it's been running for > Dividing by 5 (Or whichever the number you've set) to determine the speed of our animation. Then it's getting the decimal of the equation and then multiply the answer by 5 (Or whichever number you've set).

For example:
> Time is 32.231 seconds.
> 32.231 / 5 = 6.4462
> Now it's taking 0.4462 and times this by 5. This is now 2.231.

This will then ask the Flipbooks in the Material: "Hey, which one of you is higher than 2 but lower than 3"? In which metaphorically speaking, the correct Flipbook would raise it's hand.

So now, your Material should look like this:

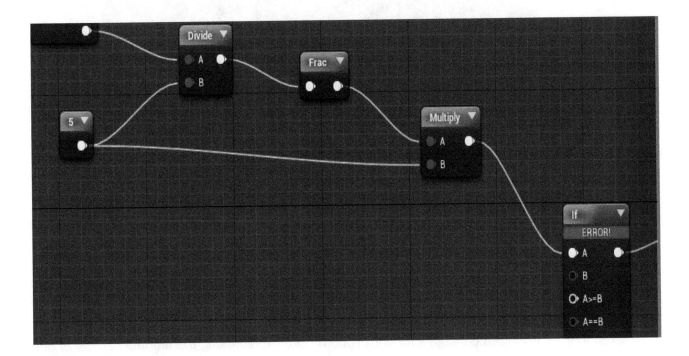

Step #10 - Let's go back to our If statement. We've filled the "A" pin, but the rest of the pins remain empty. Now it's time for us to change that. Create a Constant (Press "1" on your keyboard or search in the Library on the right for "Constant") and in the properties on the right, set the value to "1".

For our If statement, A represents Time and B represents "What Flipbook is this?". Since this is the first Flipbook in the chain, we're going to set B to one and we do this by connecting the Constant (With a value of 1) to B.

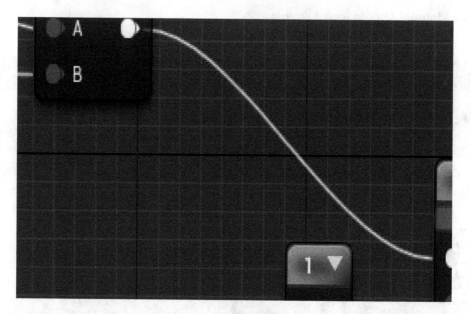

Step #11 – Grab the empty pin "A<B" (At the bottom of the If statement) and type in the search box "Flipbook". This will be the basis of our first stage of our Animation.

Step #12 – Create two constants for our Flipbook, one representing the amount of rows of our Spritesheet and the other representing our Columns (Press "1" on the keyboard or search for it from the library. The properties to alter the values are on the bottom left of your Material Blueprint).

Step #13 – Drag the empty pin of the Flipbook node ("Texture T2d") and in the search box type: "Texture Object". In the properties of this Texture Object, set the first Spritesheet.

Step #14 – Drag the empty pin "Uvs" from our Flipbook node and search for "Texturecoordinate".

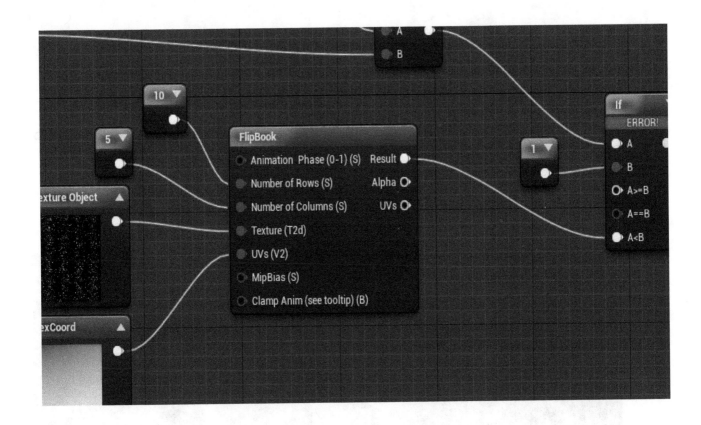

Step # 15 - Our first Flipbook is set up, but here is where we'll branch once again:

- If you have ONE more Spritesheet:

Step #1 - Copy your Flipbook and the children nodes (Ctrl + Click the nodes one-by-one and then press Ctrl + C on your keyboard (Alternatively, Right Click [Ctrl + Click] and select Copy).

Step #2 - Press Ctrl + V (Right Click [Ctrl + Click] the empty space underneath your Flipbook to create a copy of our Flipbook.

Step #3 - Click the Texture Object and in the Properties field, change the Texture to your Second Spritesheet. (Also alter the Constants for Row and Columns if need be!)

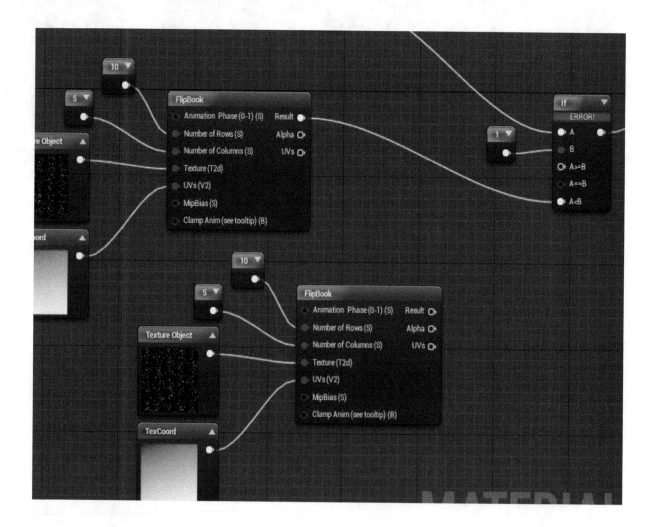

Step # 4 - From the empty Result pin of our second Flipbook, Drag and connect it to "A>=B" of the If node.. Once this is done, go to the newly filled white Result pin of our second Flipbook and also drag it to "A==B" of our if node. All of the "If" pins should now be filled.

What did we just do? - Let's take a look at our If node. Here is what it's now doing:
   - **If "A"** - This is the current time of the Material.

- **If "B"** - This is what Flipbook to play.
- **If "A>=B"** - If the time is more than or the same number as what flipbook to play, We play the SECOND Flipbook.
- **If "A==B"** - If time is the same number as what Flipbook to play, We play the SECOND Flipbook.
- **If "A<B"** - If time is LESS than the number of what Flipbook to play, we play the FIRST Flipbook.

Your Material should like this and if it does, you've just created your animated Material!

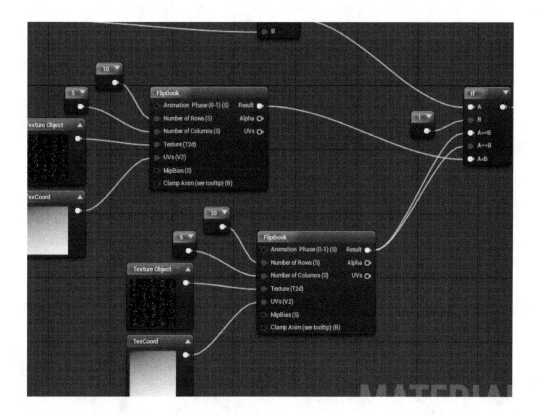

If you have MORE than two spritesheets, we're going to have to do a slightly different method! Let's rewind time to when we'd just completed our first Flipbook.

41

- *If you have MORE than ONE more Spritesheet:*

Step #1 - Copy your Flipbook and the children nodes (Ctrl + Click the nodes one-by-one and then press Ctrl + C on your keyboard (Alternatively, Right Click [Ctrl + Click] and select Copy).

Step #2 - Press Ctrl + V (Right Click [Ctrl + Click] the empty space underneath your Flipbook to create a copy of our Flipbook.

Step #3 - Click the Texture Object and in the Properties field, change the Texture to your **Second** Spritesheet. Remember to also alter the Constants for Row and Columns if need be!

Step #4 - Head back to our "If" node. We need to copy this If node, as well as the constant that's connected to B. So Ctrl + Click both the "If" node and the number "1" which we've plugged into "B". Ctrl + C (Or Right Click [Ctrl + Click] > Copy) to copy them and Ctrl + V (Right Click [Ctrl + Click] > Paste Here) to create the duplicates. Now move these to below our first If statement.

Step #5 - Connect our SECOND Flipbook's "Result" to the second "If" node's "A<B". Once this is connected, Connect the right-hand pin of the SECOND "If" node to the "A>=B" of the first "If" node and once more to the "A==B". Once this is done, on the SECOND "If" node's constant (That's plugged into "B"), change the property value to "2". (Look at this screenshot for reference!)

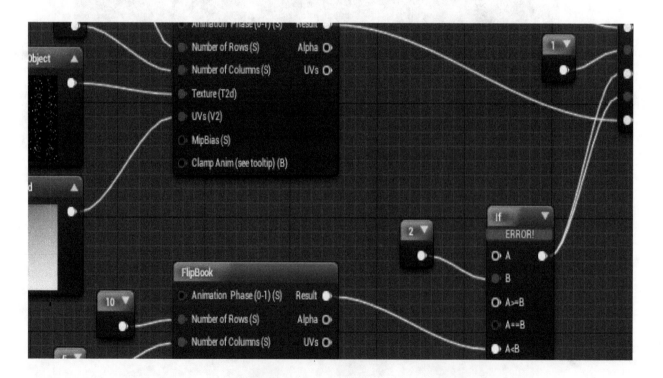

Step #6 - Our second If node is missing an A connection, but our first If node has one; It's connected to multiply. Grab the empty "A" pin from our Second If node and drag it into the Multiply we set up for time; This makes sure that all the Flipbooks run on the same time.

Step #7 - If you need more than one more Flipbook for your Spritesheet, repeat Step #1 - Step #6 until you're left with an If that has "A", "B" and "A<B" connected up and a final Flipbook that needs connecting up, then:

Step #8 - We've connected Spritesheet 1 and 2 together, but we still need to connect Spritesheet 3 (Or if you're using more then 3, you'll have 1, 2 and 3 connected and not 4 .etc). If we created another If statement, we'd have too many open pins on the If statement to work.

I mean how can you If "A<B" and "A>==B" if we're using one value? It would just confuse things.

Here's how we'll hand the final Spritesheet!

Step #9 - Copy a previous Flipbook and it's children (The rows constant, the columns constant, the texture and the TextureCoordinate) and paste it under our last Flipbook.

Step #10 - Alter the Texture to be your final Spritesheet. (Change the rows and columns if need be too!)

Step #11 - Assign the results of our last Flipbook as "A>=B" and "A==B" by dragging the results pin to the empty pins on our If statement.

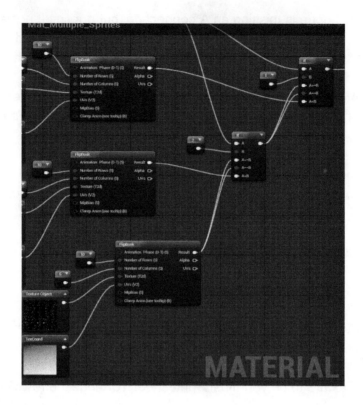

And that's the basics of Flipbooks and animations! If you're using three textures, your Blueprint should now look like this:

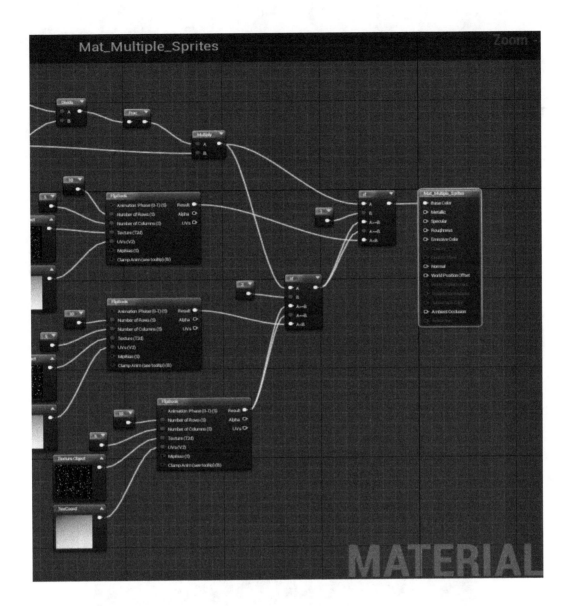

Notice how complicated it looks yet how simple it was to implement. That's the thing about Blueprints - It's very easy to look complicated, but when you trace the line along to follow what's going on, you begin to realize just how simple the Blueprints system is!

Sometimes however, they'll get so complicated that it becomes hard to find your way amongst the spaghetti lines, but we'll get to how to deal with that a bit later on!

Quick note! - Before carrying on, it might be a good time to re-mention the Emissive Colour. If your animated portal is too dark and you want it to glow, hook the first If statement into Emissive as well as base colour!

Creating our Portal!

So we've got our material ready for our Portal, but now we need the Portal! There's a few ways we can go about this, but I'm going to go with the cleanest and most organised way!

First, we're going to have to be able to see the Engine content folder in our Content Browser.

Step #1 - Head over to your Content Browser

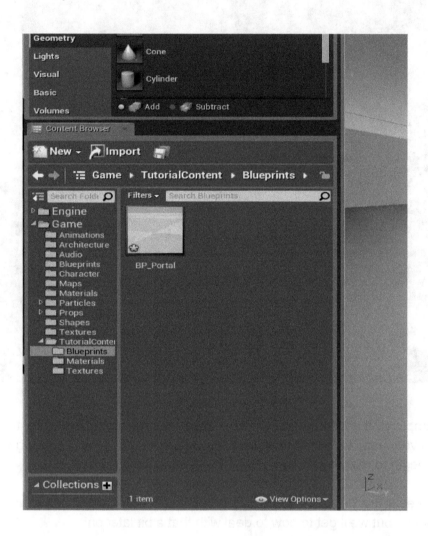

Step #2 - Click the "View Options" with the eye just before the text.

Step #3 - There will be small menu that pops up, "Show Engine Content" should be unticked. We want to see this content, so tick it and in the folder structure on the left, you should now see "Engine" above "Game".

Step #4 - Click the nice big "Engine" button on the top left of the Folder view in the content browser.

Step #5 - With Engine selected, type in the search box on the right "EditorPlane".

Step #7 - Click the EditorPlane to highlight it. Once Highlight, Right Click [Ctrl + Click] and select "Make Copy..." which will duplicate the EditorPlane. Input any name of your choosing... I've gone for "Mesh_Portal".

NOTE: Once naming your duplicated copy, the Content Browser might kick you out back into the Engine folder. If this happens, simply search in the top bar with the name you gave our copy!

Step #8 - Click and Drag your Portal mesh into the folder we created earlier in the tutorial (Or anywhere you're going to remember where it is!)

Step #9 - Once moved, Double click the mesh to open it up in the Static Mesh Editor!

So you might be wondering; *Why the heck did we just do that*?

Well… For our Portal, we need the most inexpensive mesh we can get and you can't get as less taxing of a mesh than an EditorPlane. But looking ahead into the future, EditorPlane's can't have materials assigned to them once we're in our Portal blueprint.

So we've created an EditorPlane that we can alter the Material to so that when it comes to importing it into our Blueprint! Now is the time to alter the material of our EditorPlane (Which is now called "Mesh_Portal" or whatever you have called yours!)

Step #10 - In the Static Mesh Editor, on the right you should see "Element 0" under LOD1, with "WorldGridMaterial" assigned to it.

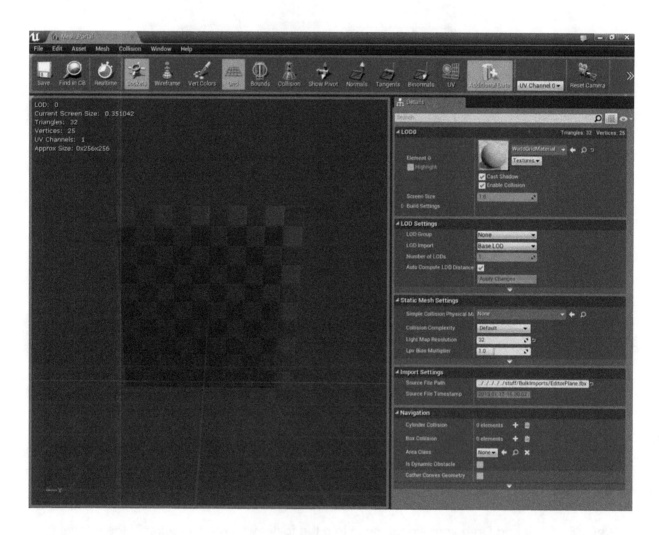

Step #11 - Where it says "WorldGridMaterial", click the little light gray arrow and in the search box that appears, type in the name of the Material you have created.

NOTE: If your Material hasn't applied very well (Falling off the screen, tiled twice or similar problems), then you'll have to go back into your Material and alter the properties of "TexCoord". Usually, enabling "Un mirror V" should solve the problem, but it may require you to tinker around with the settings inside TextureCoordinate until it fits your EditorPlane properly. Remember to Apply every time you make a change before checking the EdtiorPlane or it won't update with the latest Material properties!

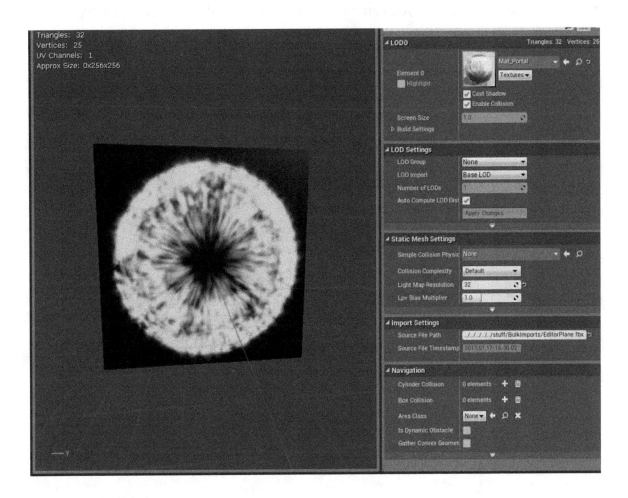

Now that our EditorPlane has our Material on it, we are now ready to begin piecing together our Portal Blueprint!

Piecing Together our Portal Blueprint

Step #1 - Go back to the Content Browser and open up your Portal BP (I've called mine "BP_Portal")

This will open up into our Components tab of the Blueprint editor. If your Blueprint hasn't opened in the Components tab, you can navigate through the different tabs on the top-right of the Blueprint editor.

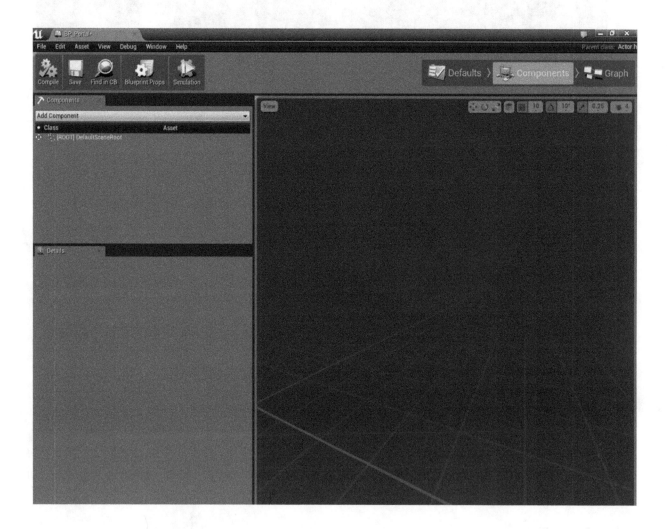

Step #2 - Under the "Compile" and "Save buttons is a drop-down menu called "Add Component". For good practice, Click this and add a "Scene". This means that if we do anything to alter the position / rotation of this Blueprint, it'll alter the 0.0.0 location of inside, which will save your butt more times then you'll realize.

Note that it doesn't matter what you call this "Scene" as it's only there to hold the actors / items / meshes that we put into the Blueprint.

Step #3 - Once "Scene" has been created, click the "Add Component" dropdown menu again. This time type in "Static Mesh" and click it. This will be our Portal.

Helpful Tip: You should now see in the hierarchy view that it says "Scene1" and the Static Mesh we've created has become a child of "Scene1". If this isn't the case for you and "Scene1" has become the child of the Static Mesh, just click and drag the "Scene1" up to where the Parent is and it'll make sure "Scene1" becomes the Daddy/Mommy of everything in the Blueprint.

Step #4 - Click the Static Mesh that has been created (Under the "Add Component" menu). If you scroll down the in the "Details" pane, you'll get to a section called "Static Mesh" with a big white box saying "Static Mesh" with a thin gray box also saying "Static Mesh".

Step #5 - Click the light gray box and search for whatever you called your EditorPlane. I called mine "Mesh_Portal".

Now the EditorPlane is in the blueprint, some of you can't see it! Well it's there! Trust me. There's just one little thing we need to do if you can't see it:

As EditorPlane's are one-sided, we're currently looking at it's butt. We want it to face the correct way! Since Unreal Engine works with Y-Axis as the front...

In the details pane, under Rotation, change the Y-Rotation to 180.0. This should flip around your Portal so it's facing the right way.

(If I were an annoying paperclip, I'd be now reminding you: Now is a great time to save so you don't lose anything! Just hit the floppy disc! You could also hit the Gear to Compile of you want to as well!)

Your Portal now exists and stands strong in your Blueprint. We're almost there!

Once thing we're going to need is a trigger box; That means when something touches the box, it'll do an action. The reason we want this is because we want the player to walk into the Portal and for them to be teleported to the next level.

Step #6 - Click the "Add Component" drop down box again and this time search for "Box" and click it.

Step #7 - In the Box properties, you'll see three widgets with red, green and blue colourings called "Location", "Rotation" and "Scale". *Put these values into X, Y, Z of Scale*:

Scale X: 0.5
Scale Y: 3.5
Scale Z: 3.5

This ensures that the box covers enough of our Portal to act as a great trigger box, without bleeding too much over so the Player would accidentally walk into when they don't want to transition.

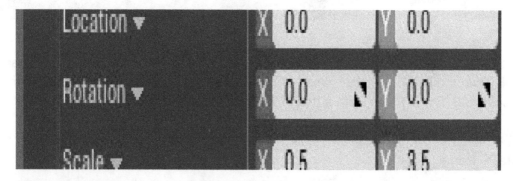

Step #8 - In the properties box above Transform, there's a section called "Variable" which a value called "Variable Name". Let's set this to "Trigger_Portal".

You should now have a Blueprint this looks like this:

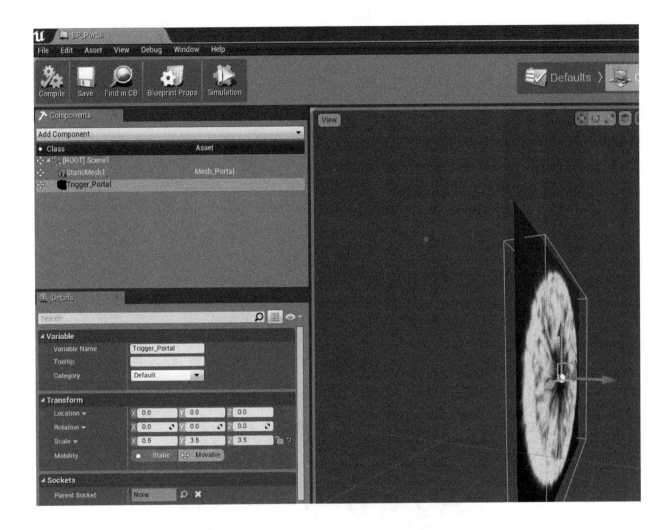

We don't want anything else to trigger our Portal to tell the level to load the next level (That would be disastrous!), so we'll need to alter the collision properties of our Trigger_Portal. To the right of our Variable and Transform settings, there's a little scroll bar that we can use to see more properties.

Use this scrollbar and scroll down until you see the section named "Collision".

Step #9 - Under "Collision", there's a section called "Collision Presets" with "OverlapAllDynamic" pre-selected. Click "OverlapAllDynamic" and replace it with "OverlapOnlyPawn". This will stop any nasty bugs happening down the line which will mess up our game!

Our portal is now almost ready! But we've got a few things more to do before it's 100% functional. What we have to do now is go back into our Level and add a place in the wall where the Portal can sit snug and tight.

Finding a Home for our Portal

Above the Content Browser, there's a section of Unreal Engine 4 called "Modes". This allows us to add geometry, lights, triggers, the lot! This part of Unreal Engine 4 is essential for anything in Unreal Engine 4 and we're going to use it right now to create a hole in the wall to place our Portal.

Under the Box with a Light in front of it, there's a number of options that look like this:
- Recently Placed
- Geometry
- Lights
- Visual
- Basic
- Volumes

What we're going to create right now is a box to take a chunk of the pre-existing wall out. We do this by creating a Geometry Box and subtracting it from everything.

Step #1 - In the "Modes" pane, Select Geometry and Click + Drag the Box into the Scene View. This will create a box into our Game.

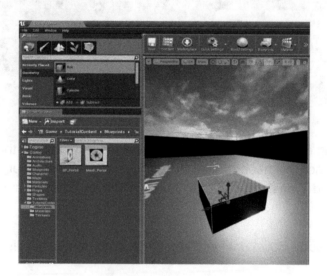

Step #2 - Click the newly created box inside the Scene View and on the right, you'll see "X - 200, Y - 200 and Z - 200" under brush settings on the right. For our tutorial, we'll need to change "Z - 200" into "Z - 240", this covers the correct part of our Portal.

Step #3 - Click the box once again and use the XYZ Gizmo to move the box INTO a wall of your choosing, leaving a little bit poking out of the wall (So it looks like a door).

TIP: (If you can't see the XYZ Gizmo, you can use the W key on your keyboard to toggle it on!)

Make sure you also align your Box so it's touching the floor (We can alter this later). Your box should now look like this:

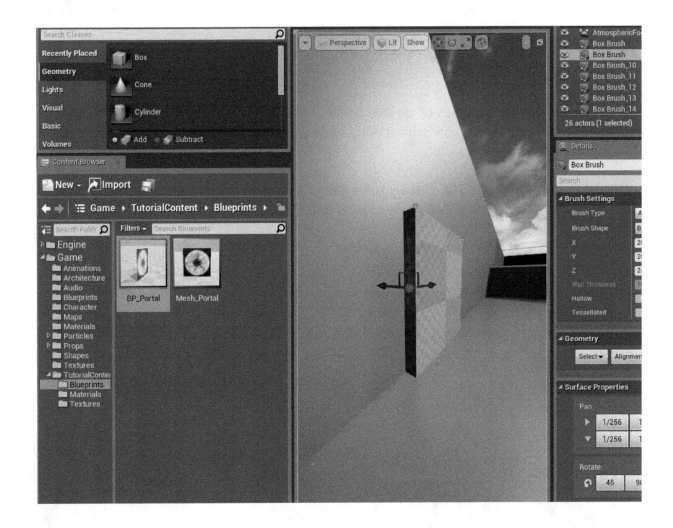

Step #4 - Back on the Brush Settings on the right, just above the XYZ values (Which we edited the Z from earlier), there's a value called "Brush Type" which is currently set to Additive. Click Additive and change this to Subtractive. You'll immediately notice the difference to your box!

If it looks like your Box has eaten some of the floor away, simply select the box again and use the XYZ Gizmo (W on the Keyboard) to raise it just above the floor.

TIP: You might need to disable the grids and snapping features to get it align with the floor perfectly. These can be found on the top bar just above our Scene View. They look like this:

In the screenshot, the Grid, Angle and Scale tools are all snapping to 10, 10 degrees and 0.25 respectively.

If your box is moving too much or too little and you can't get it just right, if you click the Orange buttons for the Grid, Angle and Scale it will disable snapping completely, so you can get the box as precise as you need it.

Unreal Engine Etiquette Tip: Once you've got your box in the perfect position, remember to re-click the Grid, Angle and Scale to turn them back on!

You should now have this or something similar:

Step #5 - Back in the Content Browser, just like what we did for our Box, Click and drag the BP_Portal (Or whatever you've called your Portal Blueprint) and drag it into the Scene.

You should now see your Portal in the game. If you can't, the Portal is the wrong way round!

To fix this: With the Portal Blueprint selected in the level (Not the Content Browser one!) - Press E on your keyboard (Or the rotator tool on the top of the scene view!) to turn on the Rotation tool and the click and drag the blue Axis of the Portal 180 degrees to the left / right. You should now see your Portal!

Step #6 - Now use the XYZ Gizmo (Use W on your Keyboard or the button on the top of the Scene View) and slot your Blueprint INTO the new doorway we've created with the box.

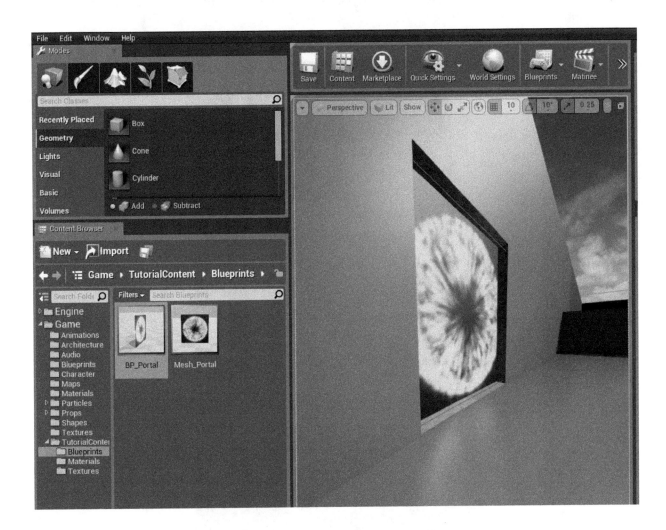

Now our Blueprint is in the Game, our Portal exists! You can have a look yourself in game by hitting the nice just play button on the top of the editor. But it's not hooked up yet, now is the time we take our venture in Blueprint Coding!

Time to Make the Portal... a Portal!

For this next step, we're going to have to alter our Character blueprint. The default for the Template we used is called "MyCharacter", however if you've already altered this, we'll be editing the "Character" blueprint (We'll get to how to create one ourselves when we delve deeper into Blueprints in this book!)

Step #1 - In the content Browser, make sure you're in the "Game" folder by pressing the giant Game folder button in the folder view.

Step #2 - In the search box, Search for "MyCharacter" (Or the name of your Character Blueprint!)

Step #3 - Double click the MyCharacter to open up the Character blueprint.

This should open up the "Graph" of our MyCharacter, but if you've loaded into the "Defaults" or "Components" tab, simply use the ribbon on the top where it says "Defaults, Components, Graph" to navigate to "Graph".

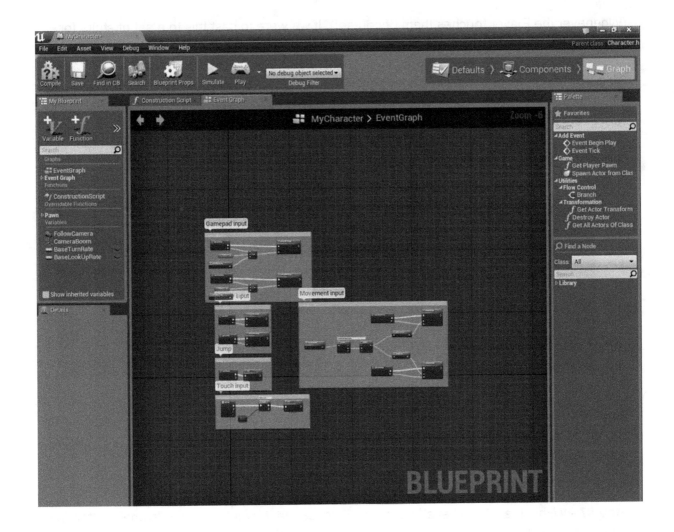

Step #4 - In an empty space of this Blueprint (Zoom in with your Mouse Wheel if you have to!) - Right click (Ctrl + Click) and in the search box that comes up, type: "Overlap" and select "On Actor Begin Overlap" which is under the "Collision" class.

What we need to do now is tell the Portal blueprint: "Hey, this dude is totally touching you!" so we're going to do something called a "Cast".

What is a Cast? - In this case, because the Cast is connected to an Event called "Actor Begin Overlap", the cast will tell whatever is connected to it that the Player is touching them

(Whenever the Player touches them of course!). If we were to cast this to a set of stairs for example, it would tell the stairs when the player is touching .etc

Step #5 - We need to establish the connection from our Portal to our Player, so from the blue pin of "Actor Begin Overlap", click the empty pin and drag to the right. In the menu that appears, type in the search box "Cast to BP_Portal" or "Cast to (Your BP Name)" and you should see "Cast to BP_Portal (Or your Blueprint Name)" appear. Click that and we have begun the connection to the Portal blueprint! There now able to talk to each other!

Step #6 - Now we're talking to the BP_Portal, we need to tell it to open the next level. So click the empty pin above "Cast Failed" and drag to the right. When the Compact Blueprint Library opens up, we want to search for "Open Level".

Step #7 - Within the "Open Level" node, you'll notice that Level Name has "None" written in it. If we click that text box and enter our Level name, our Portal will work!

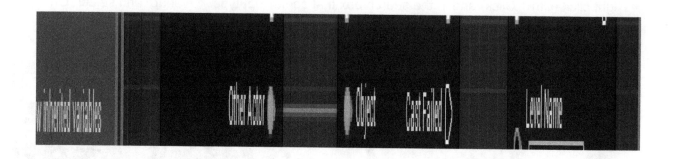

Note: Because we've done all of this through an event (Actor Begin Overlap), we don't need to hook anything else to our Blueprint. Normally, If you're not doing what you want to do through an event, it'd have to be connected to somewhere else in the Blueprint!

Now is a great time to Compile and Save! So make sure you press the gear and floppy disc at the top of your Blueprint and try out your creation by pressing the Play button above the Scene View in the Main Unreal Engine window!

There is a Better Way to Do Things!

The portal works so at this moment it's a cause for celebration! You've done your first line of code! But hang on a moment... What if we had a BP_Portal in another level, wouldn't that mean that because we can't change the Level Name in-game that it would forever load the second level?

This will make your "MyCharacter" blueprint messy VERY quickly. There's a simpler way of doing things!

Step #1 - Delete "On Actor Begin Overlap" and everything else we create after it in the MyCharacter blueprint.

I bet you're thinking to yourself - What the heck?! Why?! - But *trust* me on this one.

Step #2 - In the Content Browser, find your "BP_Portal" (Or whatever you've called yours!) and double click it to open the Blueprint.

Step #3 - Head over the Graph of the Blueprint (Use the top-right ribbon to navigate!) and add an "On Actor Begin Overlap", JUST like what we did in the "MyCharacter" blueprint.

Step #4 - Grab the empty blue node and drag it to the write. In the Compact Blueprint Library, search for "Cast to MyCharacter (Or the name of your Character blueprint!)"

Step #5 - Now, Just like we did back in the MyCharacter blueprint, Click the empty pin above "Cast Failed" in the Cast node and drag to the right and search for "Open Level".

Step #6 - In the "Level name: None", remember to change it to the name of our Second level!

Now we have a cleaner version of exactly what we did for the MyCharacter blueprint! But this makes MyCharacter a lot more cleaner and if we wanted to change the level name, we could duplicate the whole blueprint and alter the name of the "Open Level" to a different level!

But... *Dramatic Pause*... You might have noticed something when trying out the Portal...

When the level changes, the game hangs for a moment or two while it's loading the next level. To some, that might not bother them. But for most, we'll want to hide that as much as possible. How do we do that?...

...Well with a loading screen of course!

Making a Loading Screen!

To create a Loading screen between the levels, we're going to need a few things first!

Step #1 - Import the texture you want to use for your Loading Screen! (In the Content Browser > Import)

Step #2 - Right click your imported Texture and click "Create Material..."

Step #3 - Open up the Material and plug the "Texture Sample" into the empty Emissive pin so it is connected to Base Colour AND Emissive Colour - (Remember to Save!)

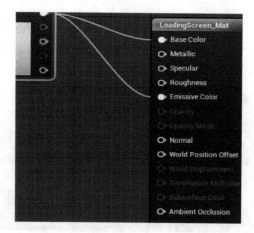

We're going to need a HUD for the next few steps. For those who don't know a HUD is what the player sees on the screen, for example a menu, the time, how many coins you've currently got .etc

A HUD is basically anything on the screen that isn't part of the game world itself but something that should be displayed on the screen.

Step #4 - Go to the Content Browser and into our TutorialContent folder (Or whatever you've called your folder) and use the buttons on the top of the Content Browser to create a new Blueprint.

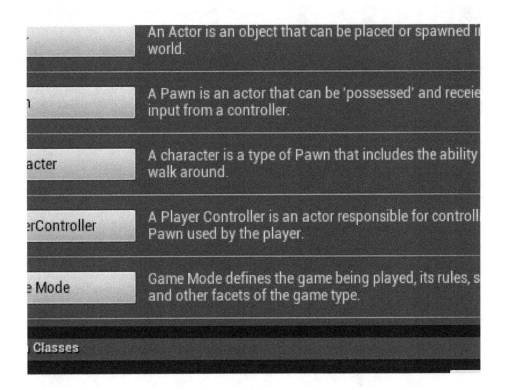

Step #5 - At the bottom of the "Pick Parent Class" window, there's a section called "Custom Classes". If we click the hollow grey button to the left of this, we'll see all the Classes we can use as a basis for this blueprint.

Step #6 - If you search for "HUD" a number of options will be revealed. The one we want is the child of "Actor" but the parent of everything else:

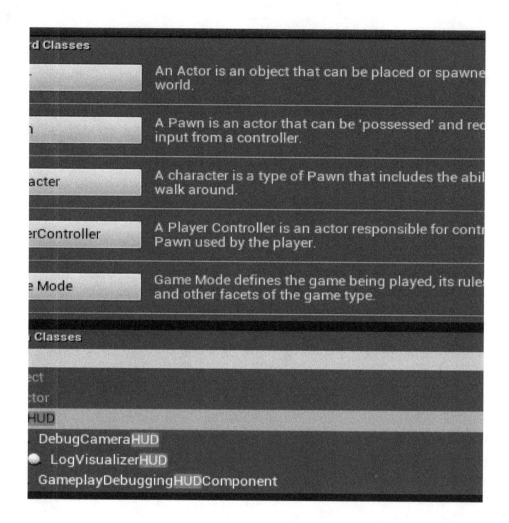

Select this "HUD" by highlighting it (Left Click) and then pressing Select at the bottom of the screen.

Step #7 - Once the blueprint is created, name it something along the lines of "HUD_Portal". This will be our HUD for this whole level.

What did we just do? - We created a blueprint. But why did we select HUD? We did this because this gives us some specific nodes which aren't available to use usually!

We're going to have to do something right now before we forget!

Step #8 - In the bar above the Scene View, you have a number of options. Next to "Quick Settings" and before "Blueprints", there's a section called "World Settings". Click this.

Step #9 - This has added a tab next to the details pane on the bottom right. If it isn't already open for you, click the tab "World Settings" and it'll appear for you.

Step #10 - Scroll down "World Settings" until you get to the section called "GameMode".

Step #11 - Where it says "GameMode Override", click the None button and select "MyGame".

Step #12 - Press the little button that sits before "Selected GameMode" to show all the properties of our "MyGame" GameMode.

Step #13 - Next to HUDClass, click the drop-down menu and set it to the HUD we just set up!

You can now close the World Settings tab (Which I *highly recommend* doing so, it's so easy to get confused when trying to alter the details of objects otherwise!)

Now it's time to head into our HUD blueprint and get it ready for the awesome in which we're about to accomplish.

Step #14 - Open up your HUD_Portal (Or whatever you've called it) from the Content Browser.

Setting up our HUD for Awesome!

Step #1 - When you've opened your HUD_Portal (Or whatever you've called it), it might open up into the "Components" tab, so use the ribbon on the top right to get into the "Graph" tab!

Step #2 - Anywhere in the Blueprint Script area, Right click and search for "Event Draw HUD".

Did you see what we just did there? - That's something we couldn't have done in a regular blueprint - It's thanks to the fact that this Blueprint is of the "HUD" class that we can access some of these important and awesome nodes!

Step #3 - Right click (Ctrl + Click) to the right of our Event Draw HUD and type in: "Make Vector2D", this is going to create something that we'll be needing later!

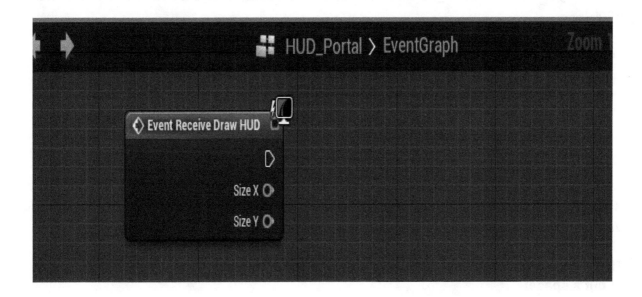

Step #4 - Drag from your Empty "Size X" pin from "Draw HUD" and connect it to the "X" of "Make Vector 2D".

Even though you can see the pins are different colours (Different properties), as you connect them, Unreal Engine automatically converts the values for you so you don't have to touch a thing.

Step #5 - Do the same thing from the Empty "Size Y" pin to the Empty "Y" pin of "Make Vector 2D"

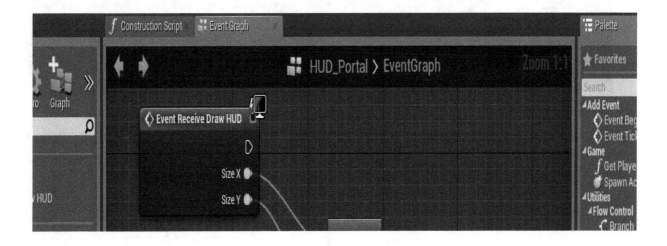

Step #6 - From the Empty "Return Value" pin from "Make Vector 2D" drag to the right and select "Promote to Variable".

What did we just do? - We created our first Variable! But *what does that mean*? Well, it's something that we can use again and again and we can also change it's values whenever we want.

This is basically the essence of variables:
> **Bool** - Yes or No's that can be stored and re-used
> **Float** - Number value (That can has decimals) that can be stored and re-used
> **Int** - Number value (That can't have decimals) but can be used to find things in Arrays
> **String** - Text that can be stored and re-used later
> **Array** - Collection of items / Ints that can be stored and re-used later

Step #7 - Click the newly created "New Var" and on the left hand side of the screen, in the "New Var" properties, change the "Variable Name" to "Screen XY" (Or "ScreenDimensions").

TIP: When using Variables, if you add a Capital letter mid-sentence, this tell the variable to put a space!

Step # 8 - Connect the empty left-hand side pin of our newly created "Size XY" variable to the right-hand side pin of our "Draw HUD".

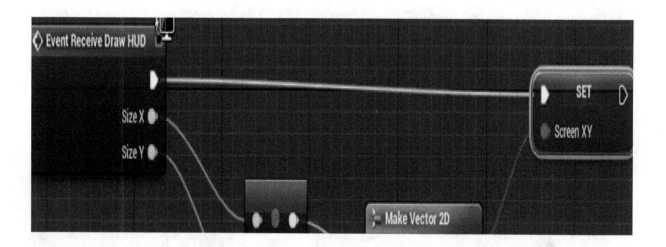

Important TIP: Everything that is in a Blueprint has to connect to an event in some way. It can connect to other "Nodes" as long as they stem from an Event in some way. Events are in red, so they're easy to locate!

When you're following along with these tutorials, you'll understand what I mean better.

Step #9 - We've set-up "This is the size of the screen" but now we need to go on a little adventure to get the player to tell the HUD to draw the loading screen. Head over your "MyCharacter" blueprint via the Content Browser.

Because we've re-created the Portal's "OnTrigger" into the portal itself, there's not a lot we have to do to the Player controller. But while digging around Blueprints and Unreal Engine 4, I have not currently found a way for an object blueprint to draw on the HUD. So I've come up with this nifty little work-a-round:

Step #10 - Inside the "MyCharacter" Blueprint (Make sure you're in Graph view!), on the left there are a few options:

At the top of this options panel, we have "Variable", "Function", "Macro" .etc - We need a variable for what we're about to do, so click the "+V", which will create our Variable.

Step #11 - A Variable gets created automatically as a Bool (It lets you alter what type of Variable it is, but a Bool is pre-selected). As a bool (Yes or No) is what we need right now, all we have to do is change the name of the Variable.

For the sake of this tutorial, set "Variable Name" to "PortalLoader".

Step #12 - Compile the "MyCharacter" blueprint. *This part is essential.* If you don't compile, we won't be able to call PortalLoader anywhere else apart from this blueprint.

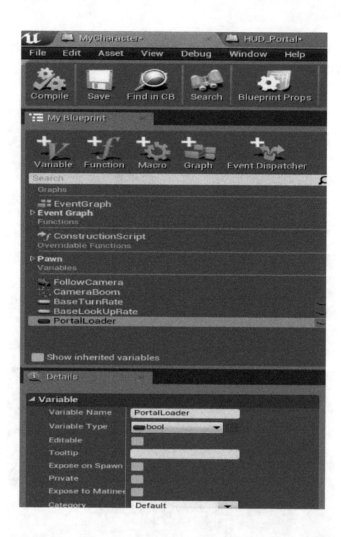

Our adventure into "MyCharacter" is now complete, it's now time to venture into our BP_Portal (Or whatever you called yours).

Step #13 - Close "MyCharacter" (After compiling!) and open up BP_Portal (Or whatever you called yours).

Step #14 - Go the "Graph" tab of our BP_Portal.

Step #15 - Right Click (Ctrl + Click) and in the search box type in "Overlap" and select: "On Actor Begin Overlap" to create the Overlap node.

Step #16 - From the Blue empty pin of Overlap, drag to the right and in the search box type: "Cast to MyCharacter" (Or your name of your Character Blueprint).

So you can guess we're calling to MyCharacter, but now you're going to learn something cool about casting!

Step #17 - From the "As My Character C" pin / The blue pin of "Cast to MyCharacter", drag to the right and type "PortalLoader". Select "Set PortalLoader".

Did you notice what we just did?! We can now edit a variable from another blueprint. What does this mean? That means we can tell things "Yes" or "No" while being somewhere else!

We can also alter numbers, or any other variables we can think of! As long as can cast to it, we can change variables! This is one of the *key elements* to scripting and Blueprints!

Step #18 - In the "Set PortalLoader" node, there is an un-ticked box in the box next to "Portal Loader". Tick it.

What did we just do? - We just did this: Overlap > Cast > Portal Loaded (Tick). To translate this to plain English: If the player is standing on me or touching me, tell them "Potal Loaded" is TRUE.

That is an important lesson, so make sure you took it on board!

So we have the Portal telling the Player that "Hey, you're touching me, Portal Loader is now true!" but we need the HUD to find out about this event happening. How do we do this? Simple! Make sure you Compile the "BP_Portal" blueprint and then...

Step #19 - Go back to "HUD_Portal" / Open it up again through the Content Browser.

You might have noticed by now that it seems like we can only "Cast" from Events, more specifically "Event Begin Overlap" nodes. But this isn't the case!

We can do lots of little tricks to be able to cast, like the one we're about to do!

Step #20 - In empty space near "Set "Screen XY", right click and search the Compact Blueprint Library for "Get Player Character". Make sure you select Character as there are a few to choose from!

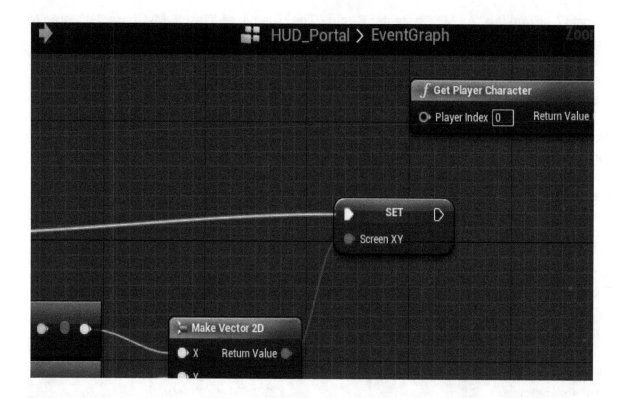

Step #21 - From the blue empty node of "Get Player Character", drag to the right and in the search box, type in "Cast to MyCharacter" (Or the name of your Character blueprint!)

We're now speaking directly to your "MyCharacter" Blueprint!

Step #22 - Before we get ahead of ourselves, as I mentioned before: You cannot trigger nodes in a Blueprint without connecting them to either an Event or the main timeline of Blueprint nodes (Which are connected down the line to an Event).

So drag the left pin of our "Cast" to the right pin of "Set Screen XY".

Step #23 - From the blue "AsMyCharacter C" pin of our "Cast". Drag to the right and type in "Get PortalLoader".

We'll need this in two seconds (Not literally), hence why we've called for it now.

So now we have a direct connection between the HUD, the Player and the Portal! But what can we do with this power?

Step #24 - From the "Cast to MyCharacter", drag the top empty pin to the right and type in "Branch".

What did we just do? - A branch is one of the most important Blueprint functions! It's basically "Is this thing happening? Yes or No?". Another way to put it would be: "This. True or False?"

Step #25 - Connect the red empty pin of "PortalLoader" to the "Condition" slot of the "Branch".

We've just done something seriously awesome! We're asking the Player "Is Portal Loader true?". Player is then asking the Portal: "Is it true?" and when the answer is yes, the Portal will tell the player to tell the HUD that it's true.

And you made that happen! Go you!

We now need to tell the HUD what we want to do if this is true…

Step #26 - From the "True" pin of "Branch", drag to the right and type in "Draw Material" and select "Draw Material Simple".

Step #27 - On the far left of the Window, where all our Variables are stores, Drag and drop Screen XY underneath "Branch". When it asks if you want to "Set" or "Get", we want to get it.

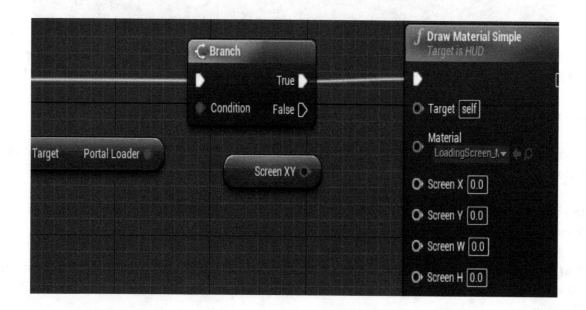

Step #28 - From the dark blue pin of "Screen XY", drag a little to the right and search for "Break Vector 2D".

What did we just do? - Screen XY is our Screen Dimensions, which we set earlier. This will determine the how big the Material has to be to fill the whole screen.As we made it into a Vector 2D earlier (To make it easier to store), it is now time to break the Vector 2D, so we can use it with our Material.

Step #29 - Drag the "X" pin of "Break Vector 2D" and slot it into "Screen W" and the "Y" pin and slot it into Screen "H".

Step #30 - In our "Draw Material Simple" node, where it says "Material: None", click the gray arrow that is pointing down and search for your Loading Screen material.

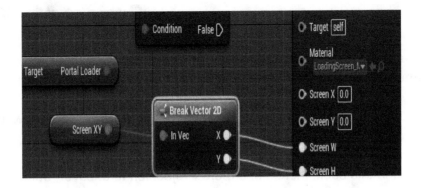

Step #31 - On the "Draw Material Simple" node, Grab the right-facing empty Pin and drag to the right. In the Compact Blueprint Library that comes up, Search for "Open Level" and just we did earlier, type in the level name of Level #2 (For me, that's "ArtOf_Example2").

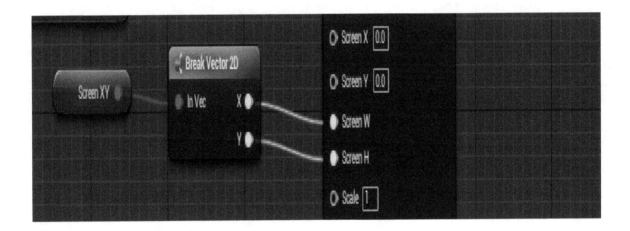

You've done it! Now only did you create a Portal, but now it'll show a Loading Screen while it's loading the next level! You rock!

Compile it and test it out if you want!

If you were using an Animated Material, I'd put a "Delay" node after the "Draw Material Simple" and before the "Open Level" and set the Delay to 2 seconds.

You did it Champ! You rock! You've made multiple Blueprints, made them talk and above all else - Made your first few steps into not only Blueprints, but in my opinion the best game engine out there! Well done!

Use your knowledge now to create another Portal coming back to Level #1 and then Level #3 .etc! You're one step closer to Mastering Blueprints! Go You!

Project #1 - Wrap-Up!

So we not only created a working Portal from Level #1 to Level #2, but we also added a Loading Screen and learned the secrets behind the Blueprints system as well as scripting in general!

We've learnt about Bools, about Unreal Engine in general and we've learnt how to make Blueprints talk to each other!

We're far from over in this book, there's one more Project left to uncover, but I hope you're feeling more confident in using Blueprints now.

We're about to enter even more exciting territory with the next Project so hang tight!

Mission #2 - First Blood II

Creating a Side-Scrolling, Multiple Character-based Adventure

Template:

Blueprint Side-Scroller

What You'll Learn:

- How to kill a Player
- Creating and switching between Multiple Characters.
- HUD
- Coin Collecting
- Cutscenes
- Basics of Applying a "Post-Process"
- Timer System

What You'll Need:

- Photoshop / Image Editing Program (For creating HUD elements)

(Extras) What You'll Need for Extras:

- Microphone
- Background Music

Let's Begin… Again!

First things first, let's fire up Unreal Engine 4 and create a new project!

If you've forgotten how to do this, when you open Unreal Engine 4, you'll be greeted with the Launcher. Simply click launch and you'll be greeted with the Project Browser.

On the top of the Project Browser, there's a HUGE "New Project" tab. Click that and scroll through the list until you find "Blueprint Side Scroller" (Don't pick "Code Side Scroller"!).

Be sure to name your Project and hit "Create Project" to begin our new adventure!

We're In!

Give Unreal Engine a moment to create the project for first time use. Once it's loaded our project, you'll notice the game looks quite a bit different to the "Third Person Blueprint" example we used in the last Tutorial.

Be sure to hit the "Play" button just above the Editor and try out what we've already got - It's pretty sweet!

The adventure we're about to embark on is going to turn this awesome project into something with even more awesome!

Take a few moments to get familiar with how the game looks and feels - You'll notice things such as the fact that everything looks like a 3D version of a 2D game. You'll also quickly notice that the player is stuck moving along the X and Y axis, to give the illusion that this 3D game is 2D. We call this "2.5D".

So once you've had a fiddle around in-game, it's time to make some major modifications!

We'll start off by adding a HUD, which we'll use to count the time as well as display how many coins the player has collected!

HUD Prep!

We'll need to create something that will become the HUD in an image editing program; If you can't / don't want to do this, I've included the HUD files we'll be using in these examples in the Project samples (Available at http://content.kitatusstudios.co.uk).

We'll need the HUD itself as well as a black and white image (Black being what ISN'T shown and white IS what should be shown.)

Here is an example of what you should end up with:

On the Left is our HUD (.PNG) and on the right is the "Opacity Mask".

The reason the black in the "Opacity Mask" covers what we don't want the HUD to draw. The White / Grey is what we is what we want the HUD to draw. We have to do this because I haven't found a way for Unreal Engine 4 to take the transparency from the .PNG and so creating a dedicated Opacity Mask ignores this fact and manually sets what we want to see.

The reason in the example images I have used Grey instead of White for the example "Opacity Mask" is so that the HUD is slightly transparent (But not too much!) which means that the Player can through the HUD and not miss any important things in the level.

While we're here, we're going to do the same thing with our Coin image (Also included in the project files).

You should now how four files: A HUD, a coin, and the two "Opacity Mask" images (One for the HUD and one for the Coin).

Now it's time to bring them into Unreal Engine 4!

HUD... HUD... And Away!

Step #1 - Just like last time, create a folder in the your Content Browser Library, so we can store all our work!

In the Content Browser, with "GAME" selected, Click "New" on the top of the Content Browser and select Folder.

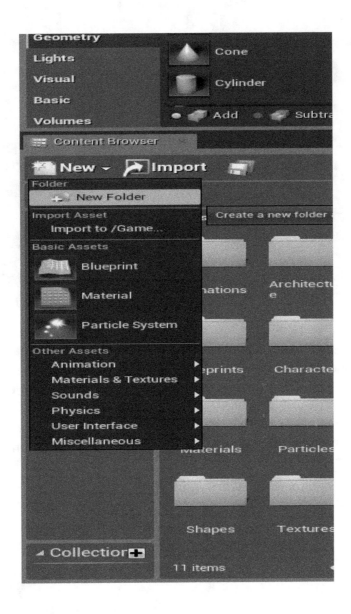

We'll call this folder "Tut_FirstBlood" (Name yours what you wish!)

Step #2 - Once we've created the Folder, it's time to open it up in the Content Browser and import all of our four HUD textures into our game!

We do this by pressing "Import" at the top of the Content Browser, then select the four textures while in our "Tut_FirstBlood" folder.

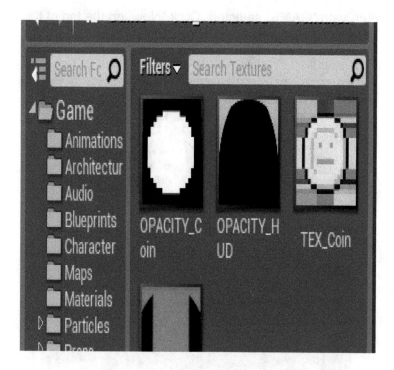

Now that our textures are into our Game, we'll need to make them into Materials for this Tutorial. BUT (And that's a big but!) we don't need to make Materials for all the textures we've just imported as two of them are actually "Opacity Masks" and not HUD elements themselves!

Step #3 - Right Click (Ctrl + Click) "TEX_Coin" (Or whatever your coin Texture is called) and select "Create Material" and do the same for "TEX_HUD". After this, rename them to "MAT_Coin" and "MAT_HUD".

Step #4 - Double Click "MAT_HUD" to open up the Material Editor for our HUD material.

We need to set a few options to make sure our HUD is in prime-shape for when we feed it into our HUD!

Preparing our HUD Materials

Now that we're in the Material editor for our "MAT_HUD", we need to set a few parameters to make sure the Material is ready for HUD usage:

Step #1 - Drag the Texture Sample that is stuck inside the "Material Inputs" node.

Step #2 - Copy the Texture Sample (Click it and Ctrl C + Ctrl V or Right Click (Ctrl + Click) and "Copy" and Right Click (Ctrl + Click) again to Paste.

Step #3 - In our newly copied "Texture Sample", Click it so we can see the Properties on the left. In the properties, where it says "Texture" with the image of our HUD texture, click the grey box and find our "Opacity_Hud".

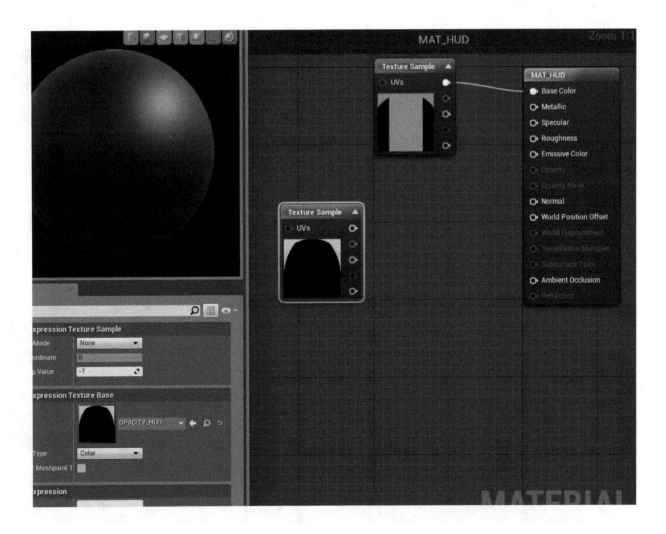

We'll be coming back to this "Texture Sample" in a little while, but we need to fix some things before the Material will accept our Opacity Mask.

Step #4 - From the filled in pin of our original "Texture Sample" (Which is connected to Base Colour), grab and connect it ALSO to Emissive. This is so the Material "Lights" itself and will still be able to be seen even in dark places.

Step #5 - Unclick all of the nodes in our Material by click some empty space within the Material Editor and you'll see some properties in the left-hand side pane.

Under the "Material" section of the properties, there's a box called "Blend Mode". As this is for something that will mainly be see-through, we need the "Opacity" node, so click the Dropdown box and select "Translucent".

Step #6 - Connect the empty pin of our "Opacity Mask" Texture Sample to the "Opacity" of our "Material Input" node.

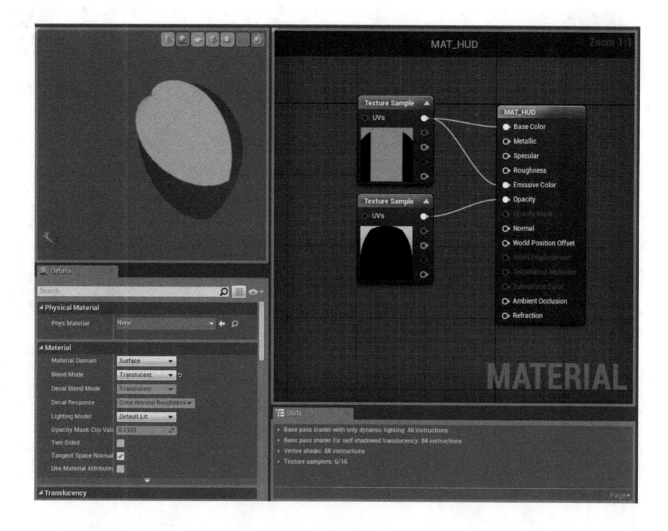

Thats all we have to do for our "MAT_HUD", it is now HUD ready! But... Before we forget...

Step #7 - Repeat Steps #1-#7 for "MAT_Coin" - (REMEMBER to save!)

Where Are We Now?

So we now have two materials, MAT_HUD and MAT_Coin. Both have been correctly set-up so they have their opacity masked out and they are ready to be placed onto our HUD.

What we'll need to do now is set up a HUD, tell the game that it's this HUD we want and put these materials into the HUD.

But we're going to do something first...

Multi-HUD!

For this example, we're going to give the player the illusion of taking control of multiple characters in order to get through obstacles.

So what we'll need to do is create some more textures and Materials to be used in our HUD to simulate the change.

I have created a Red Variant and Green Variant of the original HUD included in our "Assets" folder at http://content.kitatusstudios.co.uk - If you're using your own HUD asset, then simply use Photoshop or any other Image editing software to create a Red variant and a Green varient, so you're ending up with three HUD images: One blue variant, one red and one green.

NOTE: You don't need Opacity Masks for these variants as we'll be using the Opacity Mask from the original HUD.

Step #1 - Once created, import these into your project. From our MAT_HUD, you can clone it by Right Clicking (Ctrl + Click) and selecting "Create Copy" (Name the copies MAT_HUD2 and MAT_HUD3 in respective to the Texture names).

Step #2 - Then simply open up MAT_HUD2 and MAT_HUD3 and within the Material Editor for these two Materials, and select the "Texture Sample" which is connected into Base Colour / Emissive.

Within the properties of these Texture Samples (In the bottom left), change the "Texture" to the relevant texture "MAT_HUD2" should be using "TEX_HUD2" and "MAT_HUD3" should be using "TEX_HUD3".

You should now have a Material list that looks like this:

We now need to create the HUD and place these Materials inside, but before we do we need to tell the game that the HUD we create is the one we'd like to use for our Game.

Creating our HUD!

Step #1 - Go to the Content Browser and into our TutorialContent folder (Or whatever you've called your folder) and use the buttons on the top of the Content Browser to create a new Blueprint.

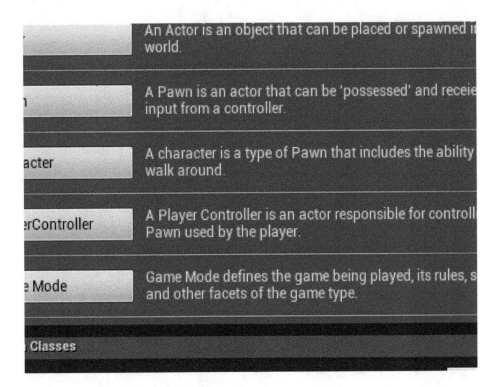

Step #2 - At the bottom of the "Pick Parent Class" window, there's a section called "Custom Classes". If we click the hollow grey button to the left of this, we'll see all the Classes we can use as a basis for this blueprint.

Step #3 - If you search for "HUD" a number of options will be revealed. The one we want is the child of "Actor" but the parent of everything else:

Select this "HUD" by highlighting it (Left Click) and then pressing Select at the bottom of the screen.

Step #4 - Once the blueprint is created, name it something along the lines of "HUD_FirstBlood". This will be our HUD for this whole level.

Now that the HUD has been created, we need to tell Unreal Engine "~~Yo Adrien!~~ Hey, Unreal Engine, this is our HUD we want to use for this Level / Game!". We can do this by setting it in "World Properties" (Which, even though makes it sound like it'll set this for every level, only sets it to the current level).

Step #5 - In the bar above the Scene View, you have a number of options. Next to "Quick Settings" and before "Blueprints", there's a section called "World Settings". Click this.

Step #6 - This has added a tab next to the details pane on the bottom right. If it isn't already open for you, click the tab "World Settings" and it'll appear for you on the right-hand side of the screen.

Step #7 - Scroll down "World Settings" until you get to the section called "GameMode".

Step #8 - Where it says "GameMode Override", click the None button and select "MyGame".

Step #9 - Press the little button that sits before "Selected GameMode" to show all the properties of our "MyGame" GameMode.

Step #10 - Next to HUDClass, click the drop-down menu and set it to the HUD we just set up ("HUD_FirstBlood")!

You can now close the World Settings tab (Which I *highly recommend* doing so, it's so easy to get confused when trying to alter the details of objects otherwise!)

Now it's time to head into our HUD_FirstBlood to begin setting up our HUD for our game!

Step #1 - Double Click your "HUD_FirstBlood" to open up the Blueprint view, if you are not in Graph view when it first opens up, use the navigation ribbon on the top right to switch from "Components" to "Graph".

Step #2 - Just like in the last project, Right Click (Ctrl + Click) the empty space within the Blueprint area and search for "Event Receive Draw HUD".

Step #3 - From the "Size X" empty pin, click and drag to the right. This opens up the "Compact Blueprint Library". At the very top (Just underneath the search box) of the Library, there's a selection called "Promote to Variable". Select that option. This will now create a Variable on the left-hand side "Variable Library".

Step #4 - Click the "NewVar" which was created the Variable Library and in the properties of this new "NewVar" change Variable Name to "sizeX".

TIP: When using Blueprints, when you start your name with a lowercase character and use an Upper-case character down the line, this will tell the engine that there is a space between the words. This sounds a tad complicated, so let's simplify it a little: If you call a

Variable "Johnrainbowlikesfood" then that's how the engine will see it, as one word. But if you called your Variable "johnRainbowLikesFood", this will tell the Engine, "Hey, this variable is called "John Rainbow Likes Food".

Step #5 - Repeat Step #3 and #4 for Size Y of the "Event Receive Draw HUD".

Step #6 - From "Event Receive Draw HUD", drag the open white pin to the left hand side pin of "SET Size X" and then set the right-hand side open pin of the "SET Size X" to the left-hand side open pin of "SET Size Y".

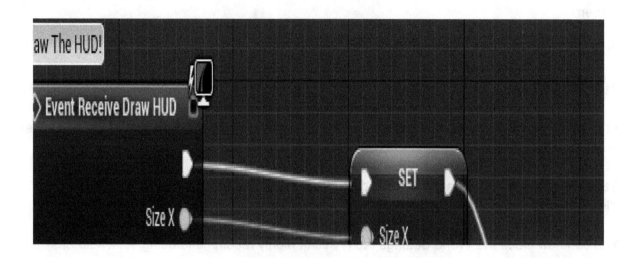

Step #7 - We're now going to have to draw our Coin material, but we want this to be on-top of our other HUD elements (Which we'll get to in a moment or two... or three).

From the empty right-hand side pin of the "SET Size Y" node, drag to the right. When the "Compact Blueprint Library" appears, search for "Sequence".

What did we just do? - We created a Sequence, which when we think about it simply is a node that says: "Hey, do this (What is connected to "Then 0") and then afterwards do this (What is connect to "Then 1"). This can be used for a lot of things, for example as you're only allowed one "Event Tick" in a Blueprint, this will let you do multiple things from the Tick, or for our Example it allows us to set the HUD material "Then 0" and THEN the coin "Then 1". Again, it sounds a little complicated, it's better to show you when it comes to things like Sequence, so we'll do just that.

Step #8 - From the "Then 1" pin of the "Sequence" node (NOT "Then 0"), drag to the right. When the CBL ("Compact Blueprint Library" pops open, search for "Draw Material Simple". This will create a "Draw Material Simple" node, which is what we'll be using to put our Coin material onto our HUD.

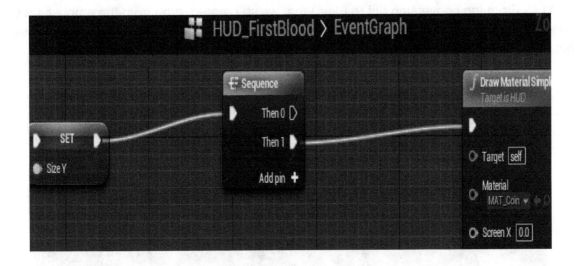

As you can see in the Screenshot just above, I've already set the properties for my Draw Material Simple, so we're going to that now!

Step #9 - If you can't make out the image for whatever reason, here are the options we need to set:

- **Target**: Leave as it is (Self).
- **Material**: Select your "MAT_Coin" Material.
- **Screen X**: Leave this for now (0.0).
- **Screen Y**: Set this to 100.
- **Screen W**: Set this to 100.
- **Screen H**: Set this to 100.
- **Scale**: Leave this as 1.
- **Scale Position**: Leave this unchecked.

We need to get the right coordinates for Screen X, so we'll use the "Size X" we set earlier and minus -250 to get the correct screen placement:

Step #10 - From the Variable Library on the left hand side of the screen, Click and drag "SizeX" into the Blueprint (Underneath the Sequence preferably). The Blueprint will then give you two options: "Get" or "Set". Since we want to get the value, select Get.

Step #11 - From the newly created "Size X", drag the empty pin to the right and in the CBL, search for "Float Int" and select "To Float (Int)".

You can now see that the turquoise "Size X" is now technically outputting a green "Float", which would fit in perfectly to our "Screen X" pin of our Draw Material Simple BUT we first need to subtract 250 otherwise it'll put our Material in a weird place.

Step #12 - From the conversion (Int to Float) that we've created, drag from the empty float pin (on the right) and drag to the right to open up the CBL. Once open, type in "Subtract" and select "Float - Float".

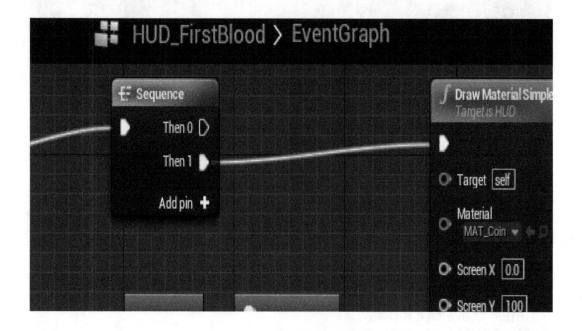

Step #13 - In our "Subtract" node, notice that our Size X is connected to the top pin of the left side and the bottom pin of the right side has "0" in it - This basically means "Subtract 0 from Size X". So where it says "0", type in "250" and connect the right hand side empty pin into our "Screen X" of our Draw Material Simple.

What did we just do? - As explained, the we minused 250 from our Size X. This is the way all equation nodes like "Subtract" work. It's the bottom number then (What kind of node it is) to the top number. So if we put 50, it would subtract 50 from our Size X.

Our coin now sits nicely on our screen, but we need to add some text to our screen. So be sure to Compile and Save our Blueprint (So we don't lose any work!) and then go back to our "Draw Material Simple" node.

Step #14 - From the empty right-hand side pin of our "Draw Material Simple" node, drag to the right and when the "Compact Blueprint Library" pops up, simply type in "Draw Text". But before we continue, there's one quick thing we have to do.

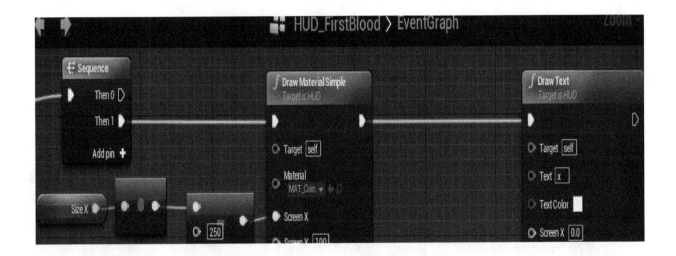

If you haven't already, go back into your Content Browser and at the bottom, there's an icon called "View Options" with an eye just before it. Click it and set "Show Engine Content". Once it's set to show the Engine content, head back into your HUD_FirstBlood.

Step #15 - Where it says Font, set the font to "RobotoDistanceField" (If you're not showing Engine content, you won't see it!)

Step #16 - Just like before, set your properties to the same as I have it. If you can't see:
- **Target**: Leave as self
- **Text**: Put a lowercase "x"
- **Text Colour**: Set to White
- **Screen X**: You can leave this as we'll set it the same way we did it before.
- **Screen Y**: Set to "120"
- **Font**: You should have already changed this to "RobotoDistanceField"
- **Scale**: 2.5
- **Scale Position**: Leave unchecked

Step #17 - Select our "Size X", the "Int to Float" converter and our "Subtract" nodes by dragging a box over them (Or using [Hold] Ctrl + [Press] Click). Once they're all selected, Copy and Paste them by pressing Ctrl + W. Drag the newly created Nodes over to our "Draw Text" node and hook up the Subtract node to our Draw Text's Screen X.

Before we do anything else, be sure to **change your newly copied subtract to "150"**, so it doesn't overlap our Coin.

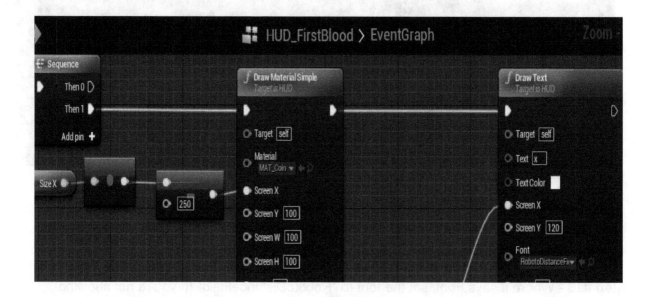

So we've got our Coin and then an x just after to separate it from what will be our score number. Before we actually put in the Score, we're going to have to set a few Variables first.

We'll also set some Variables that we'll need in the future, just to save some time.

Step #18 - In the Variable Library on the left, Create four new Variables. This is what we're going to create:

And here's how we create them!

Once you've created four variables, click the "NewVar"'s and one by one, in their properties where it says "Variable Name" - Set them to:

#1 - BlueMode
#2 - RedMode
#3 - GreenMode
#4 - Score

So now we have the four Variables named correctly, they need to be SET correctly too, otherwise they won't work like we want them to.

Go back to BlueMode's properties (By click it in the Variable Library), Just under "Variable Name", there's a part called "Variable Type". Click the dropdown box (Which should say "Int" at the moment) and set it to Bool (Red).

Repeat this for RedMode and GreenMode.

What did we just do? - We set RedMode, BlueMode and GreenMode to a Bool which means we've changed them to "Yes or No" variables (Meaning they can be either "Yes" or "No". We set Screen X and Y earlier both to "Int" which is short for Integer, which is a number, So it can be 0, 1, 2, 3, 4 .etc.

I wrote a description on the variable type's earlier, but in case you missed it:

Bool - Yes or No's that can be stored and re-used
Float - Number value (That can has decimals) that can be stored and re-used
Int - Number value (That can't have decimals) but can be used to find things in Arrays
String - Text that can be stored and re-used later
Array - Collection of items / Ints that can be stored and re-used later

All we have to do now is make sure "Score" is an Int by setting its Variable Type so. Once done, all that is left is to click the closed eye next to each Variable (See the picture just above this step) to "Open the Eye" on each four of our variables.

This means that other Blueprints can see these Variables and edit them. Why have we done this? I'll explain when we get there but for now, head back over to our Blueprint and…

Step #19 - Select your "Draw Text" node by clicking it and Ctrl + Click the nodes connected to the "Screen X" of our Draw Text. Once the "Draw Text", "Subtract", "Int to Float" and "Size X" variable are all selected, press Ctrl + W on your Keyboard to duplicate the Nodes.

Once duplicated, drag them over to just passed our original Draw Text nodes. You should now have something that looks like:

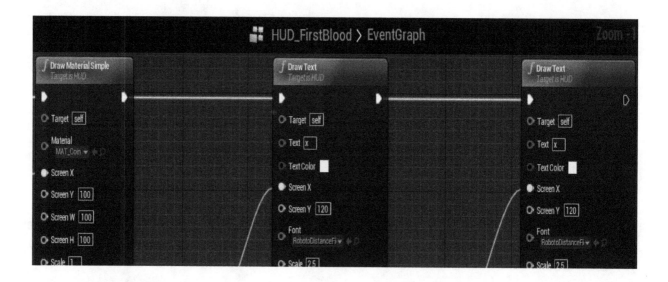

I've made one alteration (Which you should too), which is: **I've changed the Subtract to 110 instead of 150** (So the X isn't overlaying the number [Score]!)

Step #20 - Drag your "Score" variable you recently created into the Blueprint and when given the option "Get" it (Not "Set" it!).

Step #21 - From the empty pin to the right of our "Score" variable, drag to the right and type in "String" in the CBL. Select "To String (Int)".

Step #22 - Hook the empty pink pin of our "To String" to the "Text" pin of our second Draw Text.

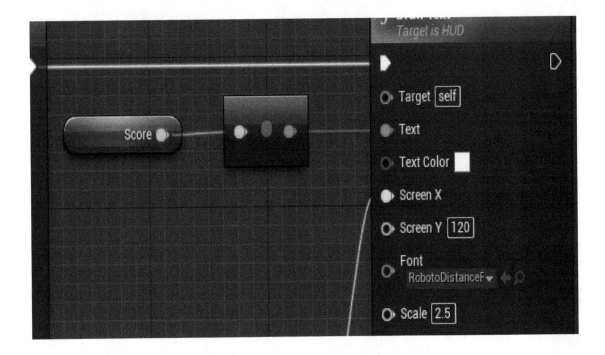

What did we just do? - You just set up a fully functioning Score counter! When we collect a coin, it will show up on our HUD so we know how many coins we have! We still need to code the coins in which we'll do in a little while but for now pat yourself on the back! We've done some awesome things! If you zoom out, look how complicated the Blueprint looks yet how simple it was to create!

If Red Player, Red HUD. If Blue Player, Blue HUD!

Now that we have our Coin and Score in the HUD, we need to set the background of the HUD. We created the Materials earlier, and now we're going to teach our HUD which HUD material to use and when!

Step #1 - In your HUD_FirstBlood blueprint, head back to the "Sequence" near the start of our Blueprint.

Step #2 - From the "Then 0" pin of our "Sequence" node, Click and drag to the right. When the "Compact Blueprint Library" pops open, type in "Branch".

Step #3 - From the Condition pin of our "Branch" node, Click the pin and drag to the left, when the CBL opens up, type in "Get Blue" and select "Get BlueMode" (The variable we created earlier).

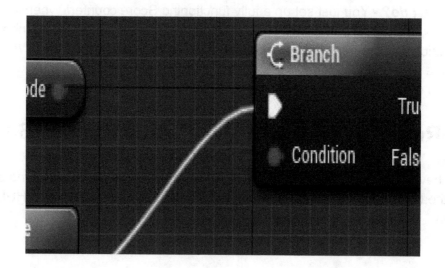

What did we just do? - As I mentioned before, a Branch is a "What if?" node. Because our "BlueMode" is a Yes or No variable (Bool), this translated to: "If BlueMode is True or False?" So we need to set what happens for each right now!

Step #4 - If BlueMode is true, we want to set the HUD to be the Blue hud we created. So from the "True" pin of our Branch, click and drag the empty pin to the right and when the "Compact Blueprint Library" opens up, type in "Draw Material Simple". This will become our Blue HUD.

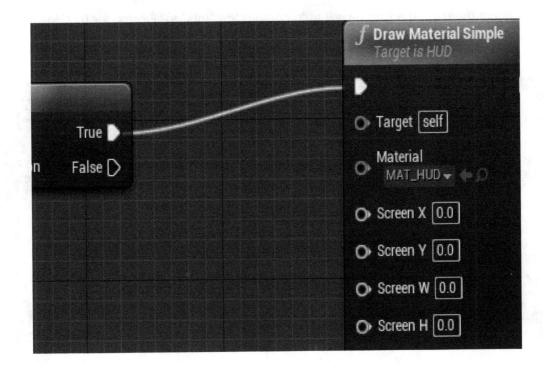

As you can see in the image, where it says "Material" in our "Draw Material Simple", I've set it to our Blue HUD ("Mat_HUD"). Do the same to your "Draw Material Simple" node.

We also need to get the Material to stretch to the screen no matter what the size of the Screen is. To do this, we're going to use the Size X and Size Y variables which we created earlier to tell our HUD to draw the Material that size. This will also automatically re-scale our HUD if the our Game's Window size is changed at any point.

Step #5 - From our "Variable Library" on the left hand side, Click and drag "SizeX" into our Blueprint (Before our Draw Material Simple) and when it asks if you'd like to "Get or Set", select "Get". Do the same for "SizeY".

Step #6 - Grab the open pin of our "SizeX" and hook it into the "Draw Material Simple"'s "Screen W" (Width of the Screen. Grab the open pin of our "SizeY" and hook that one into the "Draw Material Simple"'s "Screen H" - Screen Height.

As you connect them up, the Engine will auto convert the "Ints" to "Floats" for us (How nice of it, Thanks Epic!)

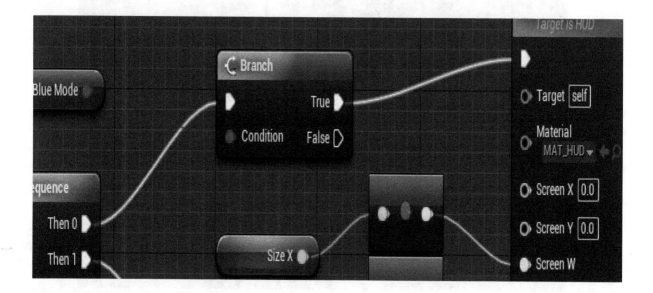

That's all we need to do for our BlueMode. It won't show up in-game yet though (We'll set that in a little bit!) but we now need to set up our GreenMode and RedMode!

Step #7 - Ctrl + Click all of the nodes we just created after the "Sequence" ("Branch", "Draw Material Simple", "SizeX", "SizeY" and their converters) but leave the "BlueMode" node. Once all have been selected (Apart from "BlueMode"), Press Ctrl + W on your Keyboard to duplicate them. Drag them above what we've just created.

Step #8 - From the "False" branch of our original "Branch", drag it into our left-hand side input pin of the second "Branch".

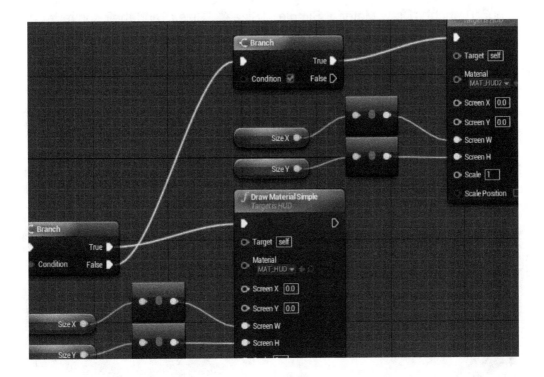

Step #9 - Where we originally set the Material to "Mat_HUD", we need to set the Duplicated version to the Second HUD image, so where it is "Material" in our Second "Draw Material Simple", click the drop down box and search for "Mat_HUD2".

Step #10 - Our second "Branch" doesn't have a condition yet. So we need to set one (Otherwise, the Blueprint is asking "What if…" and not thinking of anything else!) - From the Variable Library on the left hand side, Click and Drag "RedMode" into the Blueprint, next to our Second "Branch" and when asked, select "Get" instead of "Set". Once it's in the Blueprint, simply hook it up into the "Condition" of our Second Branch.

Step #11 - That's all we've got to do for "RedMode", now all we have to do is duplicate our "Branch" and everything after again for one last time.

So select your "Branch", "Draw Material Simple", "SizeX", "SizeY" and their converters) by Ctrl + Clicking.

Once all are selected, Press Ctrl + W on your Keyboard to duplicate.

Once Duplicated, drag above what we've just created and we'll make some final adjustments to compensate for our "Green" material.

Step #12 - Just like before, Drag the "False" pin from our Second Branch to our newly created Left pin of our third "Branch".

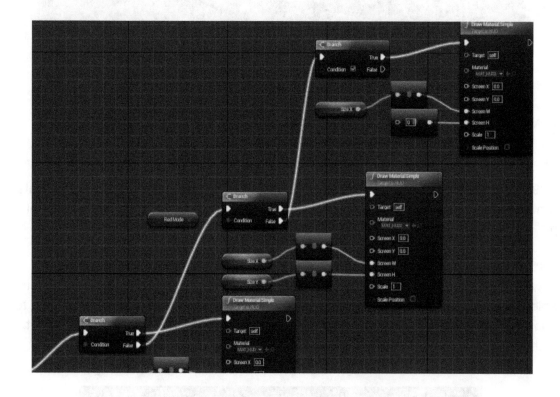

(Note: In the image, I forgot to copy over Size Y and this left an incomplete Int to Float. Copying any of the "SizeY" we've already placed down and connecting it to the open Int pin with a zero after will fix the issue!)

Step #13 - Just like before, In our third "Draw Material Simple" we need to change the Material to "Mat_HUD3" (Instead of "Mat_HUD2"). We also need to add-in the "GreenMode" condition.

See if you can do that without an explanation how.

It's really simple, and it'll help you begin your adventure in Blueprints without Tutorials. If you get really stuck, just back-track to how we already did it a few steps ago.

Step #14 - For the sake of keeping a HUD on our screen no matter what, Where it says "False" on our third "Branch", drag to the right and when the "Compact Blueprint Library" opens up, type in "Set Blue" and select "Set BlueMode".

Step #15 - Click on the little box in our "Set BlueMode" node which isn't ticked to tick it, which makes "Set BlueMode" true.

This means that if the screen isn't Blue, it isn't Red and it isn't Green, it should set Blue to true so it'll display the Blue screen.

Now let's take a look at our Blueprint:

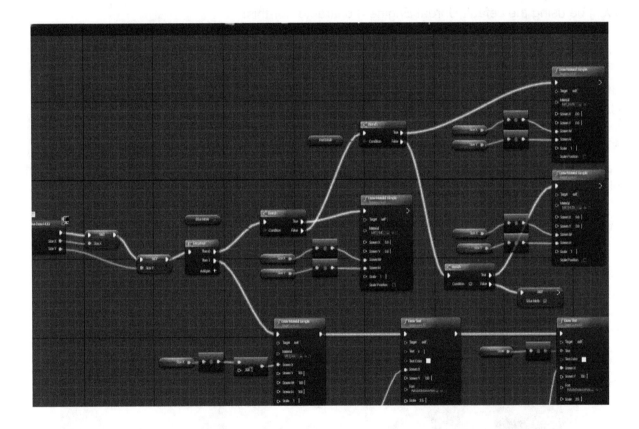

Look at how complicated it looks but how easy it is to follow now we understand what it does. Our HUD is now complete and now all we need to do is set up some gameplay specific events to make the HUD change about!

You've done a great job, well done! **REMEMBER TO SAVE AND COMPILE**.

Player meet HUD…!

Now that we have our HUD set-up, we need to be able to control our HUD from the MyCharacter blueprint (Default Character blueprint from the Project Template).

If you're not using the project template, then when I mention "MyCharacter", I'm talking about your Character blueprint.

What we're going to do before anything is set-up the Character blueprint to give off the illusion of using Multiple characters, when in reality we're just using one. Don't worry, each character will have their own unique properties.

We'll be using the default Unreal Engine 4 character for this!

First things first:

Step #1 - Open up the "MyCharacter" blueprint. You can do this by clicking Game folder in the Content Browser and searching for "MyCharacter".

If it doesn't automatically load into the "Blueprint" section, (As always) use the top-right ribbon to navigate to the "Graph" tab. If you're in the "Component" tab or "Defaults" you're not in the right place!

We're about to add this to our MyCharacter Blueprint:

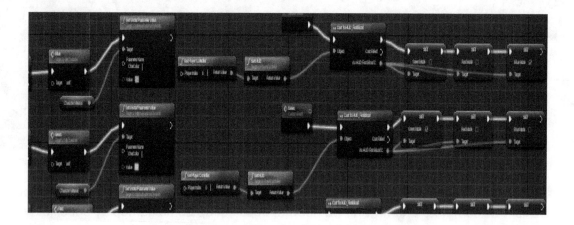

It looks a bit daunting but as we've seen time and time again, looks are very misleading with Blueprints, it's actually rather straight forward when you understand what you have to do.

The first thing we need to do is tell our "MyCharacter" blueprint that the Material that is applied to the "Mesh" (The player character) can easily be changed and altered. To do this we need to venture into unexplored territory (Or rather territory we haven't touched on in this book so far)!

Step #2 - While looking at our Event graph (Blueprint) of our "MyCharacter" Blueprint, just above the Blueprint area, you should see a tab that isn't currently open called "Construction Script".

If you can't see it, it is located here:

Once you've found the "Construction Script" tab, click it to open up our "Construction Script" Blueprint.

Just what is a "Construction Script?" - Every "Class" Blueprint has a Contruction Script, to sum it up in as little words as possible, a "Construction Script" is where you can set-up anything before everything else happens in the game. You can also use them for editor tasks (Procedural creation .etc) - But we'll go more into detail some other time!

For our example, we'll be telling the game that the Material on the player can be changed, and that needs to be done as soon as possible, hence why we're using the Construction Script.

Step #3 - Once in the Construction Script, you'll see a purple node called "Construction Script", this is our base node and everything has to come from here.

From the empty pin of the "Construction Script" node, drag to the right and in the CBL that pops up, type in "Dynamic" and select "Create Dynamic Material Instance".

Step #4 - In the "Create Dynamic Material Instance" node, on the left side there is an empty "Target" pin that is coloured light blue. We need to use this to tell the Blueprint that it's the player Mesh that we need to alter the Material for.

So click the empty pin next to "Target" and drag to the left. When the Compact Blueprint Library opens up, type in "Mesh" and select "Get Mesh" when it comes up.

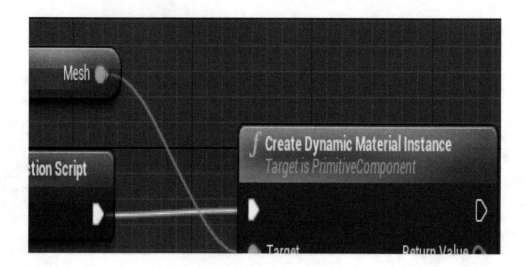

What did we just do? - We have told the "Construction Script" to tell the Blueprint that the Mesh (Player character)'s Material 0 (Element Index) [This is where all of the Material information is stored in the Default character] can be changed in-game.

What we need to do now is set this as a Variable, so that we can reference this action in our main Blueprint. We do this by…

Step #5 - From the "Return Value" empty in of our "Create Dynamic Material Instance", drag to the right. When the CBL shows up, click the option "Promote to Variable". Within the Variable Library on the left hand side, click our "NewVar" and change the Variable Name to "characterMat".

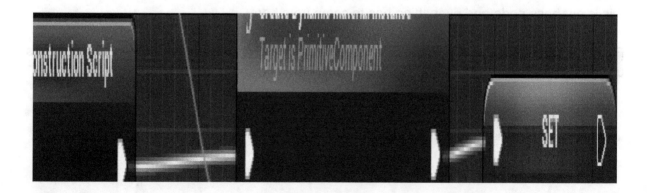

That's all we have to do for the Construction Script. Now that it tells our Blueprint to let us modify the Material and given us the Variable to do so, we need to head back into our "Event Graph" and add some things to our Blueprint!

Step #1 - In our Event Graph, in an empty space Right Click (Ctrl + Click) and type in: Custom Event. When given the option, select "Custom Event..." and name our Custom Event: "Red".

Step #2 - Repeat Step #1 for a Custom Event called "Green". Once created, Repeat Step #1 again for a Custom Event called "Blue".

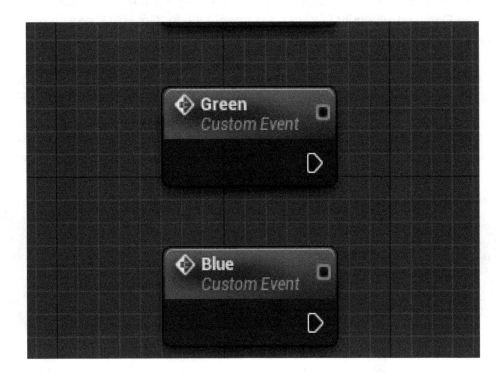

This will be how we tell the HUD to activate.

Step #3 - We need to cast to our HUD and the way we're going to be able to do that is by Right Clicking (Ctrl + Click) and when the CBL opens up, type in "Player Controller" and select "Get Player Controller".

Step #4 - From the empty "Return Value" pin from "Get Player Controller", click and drag to the right. When the Compact Blueprint Library pops open, type in "Get HUD" and select the "Get HUD" option.

Step #5 - From the empty "Return Value" pin of our "Get HUD" which has been created, Click and drag to the right. When the CBL opens, type in "Cast" and select "Cast to HUD_FirstBlood".

We're now speaking to our HUD! Remember how we gave it specific variables (Yes or No's) and various "If this variable is true do this…" branches? We're going to put them to use now!

Step #7 - Now that we're taking to our HUD, we need to tell it that we want "RedMode" to be true but everything else to be false.

So from the "As HUD First Blood C" blue pin of our "Cast". Click and drag to the right. When the CBL opens up, type in "GreenMode" and select "Set GreenMode".

This will create a "Set GreenMode" which is already set to "No". This means if "GreenMode" is already set to True, this will tell the HUD that "GreenMode" is now false.

Step #8 - From the "As HUD First Blood C" blue pin (Which is now filled in, but ignore that fact), click and drag to the right again and this time type in "BlueMode". Select "Set BlueMode".

Step #9 - When created, drag the "Set BlueMode" node to just after the "Set Green Mode" and connect their white pins together, leaving the right-hand side pin of "Set Blue Mode" ready to be connected into our "Set RedMode" when we create it.

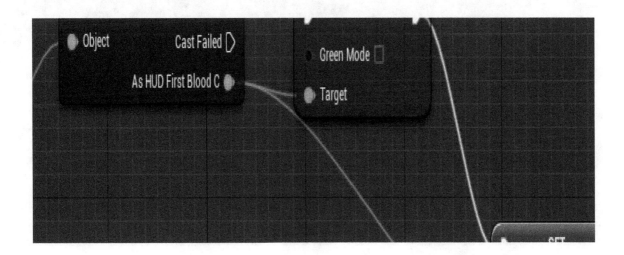

Step #10 - By now, you should be able to guess what to do next. If not, that's not a problem. Drag from "As HUD First Blood C" and when the CBL opens up, this time type in "RedMode" and select "Set RedMode".

Drag the newly created node to the end of the "Set" chain (After "Set GreenMode" and "Set BlueMode") and connect it to the Chain.

This time, RedMode needs to be set to true, so in the "Set RedMode" node, where it has the red pin then "Red Mode" and an empty box, click the empty box to set "Set RedMode" to true.

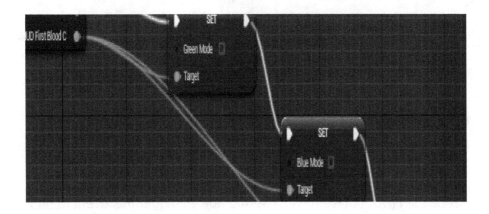

What did we just do? - When you look at our Chain which we've created (From "Cast") it goes: Set Green - False > Set Blue - False > Set Red - True. This has told the HUD to turn off the Green HUD and Blue HUD but turn on the Red HUD.

Step #11 - What we need to do now is repeat Step #3 - Step #10 with GreenMode in mind and once again with BlueMode in mind. You should eventually have something that looks like this:

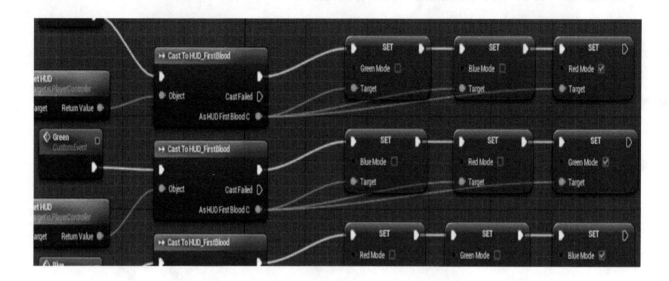

Here is an up-close version of the "Set" Nodes, just in case you need a hand:

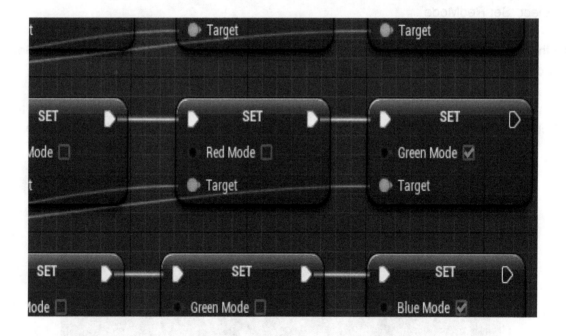

So we have set-up the HUD, but we haven't set-up how to trigger this event to happen. We have a Custom event connected to each one (Red Custom Event sets Red to true, Green Custom Event sets Green to true .etc) but we don't have anything to trigger the custom events. So now is the time we're actually going to create the event that sparks these events off.

Let's Control the HUD and Player!

We have a HUD and a system within the Player to switch the HUD when we want it to, but we need to activate this change now. We also need to change the Player colour (Which we set up earlier).

This is the part where it all falls together.

Step #1 - I'm going to be binding the different colours to different keys (Num 1, Num 2, Num 3). If you want to use a Controller, when I mention the keys, simply use whatever buttons you please (Such as "Gamepad Face Button Top" .etc).

So once you know the keys you'd like to use, Right click (Ctrl + Click) anywhere in your "MyCharacter" blueprint. When the Compact Blueprint Library opens up, Type in the Key of your choice, For example mine is the number "1", so I'll type in 1. You'll see the key you want come up under Key Events in the CBL. So select the key you want and it'll create an event with the name of the key as well as "Pressed" and "Released" nodes.

Step #2 - We need to fire the events we created. As 1 is going to be my "Red" event, all I have to do is drag from the empty "Pressed" pin of my 1 node and when the CBL opens up, type in: "Red" and select the Red that comes up like this:

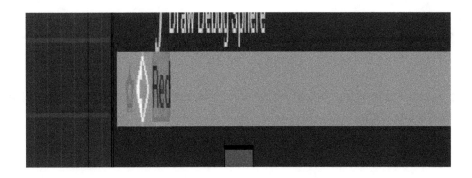

Step #3 - From the "Red" calling event which has been created, the top-right white pin can be used to set the colour of the character (So it will change the colour as the HUD is changing).

But even though dragging from the white pin and typing in "Set Vector" in the CBL would create a "Set Vector Parameter Value", it wouldn't actually create the correct Node in which we need. Even though it shares the name with the Node we want, it's actually very different.

So how do we get the right node?

Simple!

On the left hand side of your screen, you'll have your "Variable Library" (Which we've used a few times now). Inside the Variable Library, there's a variable called "characterMat" (In which we created in the Construction Script.

Simply drag the Variable into our Blueprint space and when it asks if you'd like to "Get or Set", select Get.

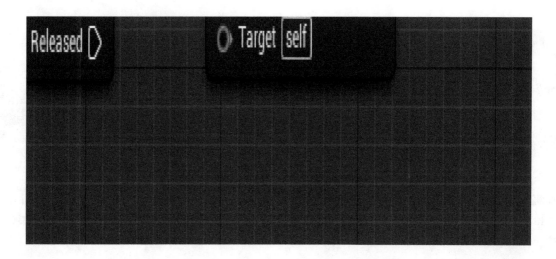

Step #4 - From the blue pin of our mini-"characterMat" node, click and drag to the right. When the Compact Blueprint Library opens up, type in "Set Vector" and select "Set Vector Parameter Value".

Once the "Set Vector Parameter Value" node has been created, connect it to the "Red" event which we created a step ago.

Once it's connected, Within the node, you'll notice a "Value" property which is currently set to Black. Because this is our Red event, we want our character to be Red.

So click the Black colour and it'll open a colour wheel. From this wheel, select a Red colour (Make sure it's red (Check all the settings of the Colour Wheel!)

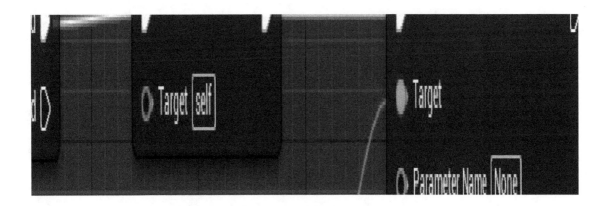

Step #5 - Repeat Steps #1 - #4 but for your other Key and Colour (Search for event "Green" instead of Red and set the colour Green. Once repeated, do it once more for our Blue colour. You should now have something along the lines of:

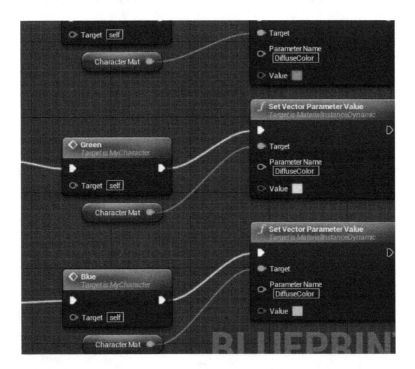

What you might notice is that in my "Set Vector Parameter Value" nodes, my ParameterName is "DiffuseColor" - That's because it is the default Parameter name for the default UE4 character's colour.

The parameter we need to change is in fact called "DiffuseColor" - So be sure to set your Parameter names (In "Set Vector Parameter Value" to this or it won't work!

So now, **compile and save**. If you try out your game, Your character and HUD will change colours when you press the buttons in which you've set!

Great work!

We're almost done but there's still a few things left to do before we can call it a day!

Give the Player Different "Powers"!

Now that we have set-up the Player's colours and the HUD, we want to give each player a different power, so Players will want to change between them!

What we're going to do is set-up ONE of the Player colours (The red one) to be able to jump higher than the rest. The other two player powers? I'm going to leave that for you to use your power of Blueprints and your imagination to come up with.

Here's is how we give the Red player the higher jump but keep it to the Red player.

Step #1 - Within the "MyCharacter" blueprint, Find the chain in which we use the Key to set off the "Red" event. In this chain, after "Set Vector Parameter Value", Click the empty white pin and drag to the right.

When the Compact Blueprint Library opens up, type in "Jump" and select "Set Jump Max Hold Time".

Step #2 - Now copy this "Set Jump Max Hold Time", and paste it twice. Connect these two copied ones to the ends of the "Green" and "Blue" key chains that we made.

Step #3 - Keep the "Blue" and "Green"'s "Set Max Jump Hold Time" at 0 but change the "Red"'s to "0.5".

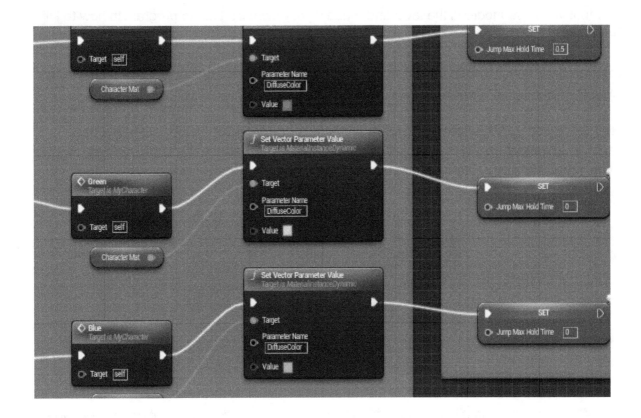

That's all we needed to do. As long as we reset the values in the other Events, it will seem as if the selected "Character" has the power when the others don't!

Step #4 - Use what you've learned to create special "Powers" for the Green Character and Blue character.

And now, once you've done that. I will give you the task of modifying your level and creating your own level. Use your imagination to modify the level in a way which will need each power individually.

Also, when you create your level, be sure to add pits in which your Player can fall into a die.

Once created, you may proceed to the next Chapter!

To Kill a Player / Coins, Coins, Coins!

Now that you have modified the level and made it your own, it's time to program in how to kill the Player.

To do this, we need to open up our "MyCharacter" blueprint once again, and this time, we're going to create a new variable.

Step #1 - Open up "MyCharacter" once again and in the "Variable Library", create a new Variable. Set it to a Bool (Red) and call it "Allow Input". Make sure to click the eye next to it's name in the "Variable Library" as this is a Variable that other Blueprints will need to see!

Step #2 - Save and Compile the Blueprint. Once Compiled, Click AllowInput (In the "Variable Library" and in the properties (Where we set the variable name), Scroll down until you find "Default Value" and make sure it says "Allow Input" and then has a tick at the end. This means "Start the game with this true!"

Step #3 - In your MyCharacter blueprint, Find ALL the events within your Blueprint, apart from the Custom Events we created (But do count the key presses!).

Now for every every, you're going to Right Click (Ctrl + Click) and select "Branch" (You can copy and paste it to save time) and hook the Event into this Branch and then the "True" to whatever the Event was originally connected to. The condition for these Branches, should be "AllowInput" (You should have figured out how to get a Variable into your Blueprint by now).

Example:

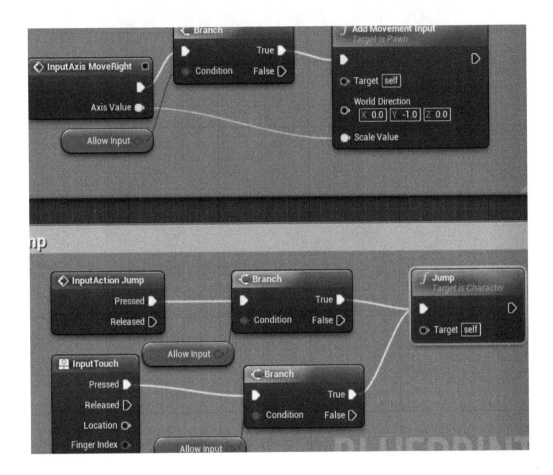

In short: Every time there is a button pressed, we want to make sure we have permission to continue. Naturally, if you're dead, you shouldn't be allowed to move around, so we're going to take away input.

(Make sure to add it to your key press "Num 1, Num 2, Num 3" as well!)

Step #4 - Now that we have added this "Can the player move?" condition to every input of "MyCharacter", it's now time to add a triggerbox into our level. Find somewhere where the player should die if they get to. Be it a pit or some spikes.

Once you've found a place, remember how we created a Box in the very first example? If we go back into the "Modes" panel at the top-left of our Unreal Engine, and we select the "Volumes" tab, if we scroll down we can find a box called "Trigger Volume". Select this and move it / Scale it into position in your pit / Over your spikes.

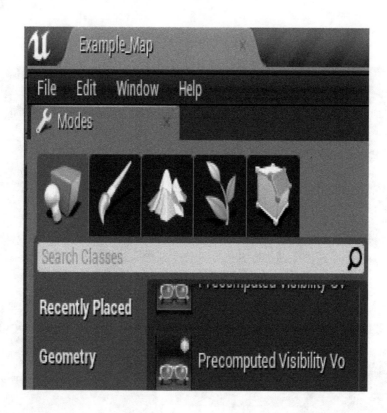

Step #5 - Once you've placed the "Trigger Volume" (And set it into the correct Position / Scale, Make sure it's selected and in it's properties, scroll down until you get to "Add Level Events for Trigger...". Click this and then select "On Actor Begin Overlap".

This will open up the Level Blueprint.

Step #6 - From the "Actor Being Overlap" node, grab the empty blue pin next to "Other Actor" and click + drag to the right. When the CBL opens, type in "MyCharacter" and select "Cast to MyCharacter".

Step #7 - In the "MyCharacter" node, Grab the blue pin for "As MyCharacter C" and Click + Drag to the right. When the Compact Blueprint Library opens, type in "Allow Input" and select "Set Allow Input". Make sure there is no tick in this node.

Step #8 - From the empty right hand side white pin of "Set Allow Input", Click and drag to the right. When the CBL appears, type in "Delay" and select "Delay".

Step #9 - From the "Delay" node's right-hand side White pin, Click & Drag to the right and in the CBL, type in "Open Level".

What did we just do? - Looking at the chain: If Player touches the Trigger Box, He can no longer move and after 0.2 second load level "None". Because we haven't set a level, it will reload the current level.

So not only did we create multiple characters with multiple different abilities, but we created a "Death trap". All we need now is the Coins. And I'll let you do that, without any help from me.

Yup, that's right. I'm taking the training wheels off and letting you explore Unreal Engine on your own.

If you don't manage to create the Coin, I've included it within the Content pack at http://content.kitatusstudios.co.uk but if you've followed this tutorial close enough, you should be able to figure out on your own what to do.

Project #2 - Wrap-Up!

You did it, Champ! Not only did you create a working Portal system in Example #1, but you rocked the World of blueprints in Example #2 by modifying Materials and HUDs all within Blueprint!

Well done!

As you might have noticed, towards the end of Project #2, I was showing you less images and getting you to do a lot more without my help.

Why did I do this I hear you ask? To help you get started on Blueprints without any help! I hope it paid off, but if it didn't - Shoot me an email and I can help anyway I can!

If you've forgotten, here's my email: contact@kitatusstudios.co.uk

I hope you enjoyed this example and please email me with how your final project looks, I'd like to see what powers you came up with and level layouts!

End of Book #1

We did it! We really did it! We created some truly awesome things and hopefully you learned some really cool stuff, so you can begin your adventures into Blueprints without me.

I hope you've learnt thanks to this book and as I've mentioned before, if you have any questions, problems or you want to show me what you've done thanks to this book, ship me an email at: contact@kitatusstudios.co.uk

Thank-you for reading and supporting this book and be on the look-out for Book #2 in the future, which will cover AI & Multiplayer!

- Ryan Shah, Project Lead @ Kitatus Studios

Mission #1 - Title Screen

Creating a Title Screen and Options Menu!

Template:

Third-Person Blueprint

What You'll Learn:

- How to use Unreal Motion Graphics
- How to set options in Unreal Engine 4

What You'll Need:

- Background Texture (For Title Screen) [1280 x 720 or 1920 x 1080]

[Extras] What You'll Need:

- Animated Material (At least 720p would work perfectly)

Let's Begin!

Hello again one and all and welcome to the next installment of Master the Art of Unreal Engine 4 - Blueprints; Where we will be covering lots of little goodies to help boost your Unreal Engine 4 knowledge.

Today we're tackling a title screen, using the (At the time of writing) still experimental tool: "Unreal Motion Graphics". This tool is (Again, at time of writing) still in it's infancy but it's power is leaking out of the sides (Not literally, of course!) - You can do so many things with Unreal Motion Graphics (Such as HUD, Menus and so much more!) - Once you've read through this mini-tutorial, you could even go back to Book #1 and compare UMG to the classic way of creating a HUD!

I'm so stoked to be showing you the ropes of UMG so I am just going to dive straight into things! Are you ready to learn even more Awesome stuff?! Hensin A-Go Go!

Step #1 - Create a new Unreal Engine project (Make sure it's on at least Unreal Engine 4.4.1, anything earlier then version doesn't have Unreal Motion Graphics!)

[NOTE: It really doesn't matter what project you use as a template, but I recommend the "Third-Person Blueprint" template as that is what I'll be using for this!]

Now you should have something similar to this screen:

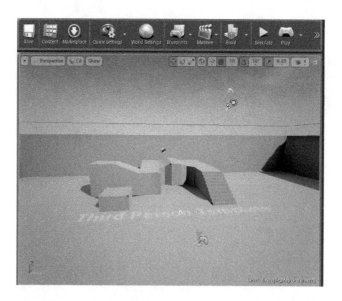

Doesn't that feel like home now? It never gets old seeing this screen!

Before we carry on, if you're living in the present time (And not in the distant future!), you'll need to activate Unreal Motion Graphics (As it's currently an experimental feature!). To do that:

Step #2 - Go to Edit (In the top-left of your Unreal Engine window, next to File) and select "Editor Preferences".

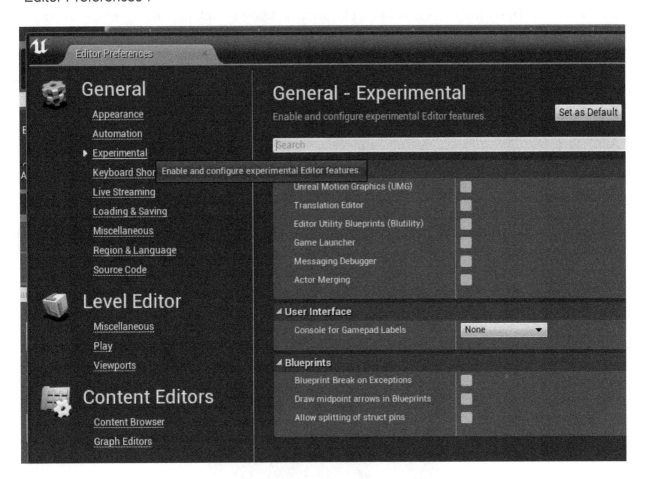

Step #3 - In the "Editor Preferences" window, click "Experimental" which is under the General header, which will open up the Experimental section.

From here, you can see "Unreal Motion Graphics (UMG)" on the right. Currently it's unticked. All you have to do is click the empty box to activate it (Make sure the box is filled in to signify it has been activated!)

Step #4 - Once you have activated "Unreal Motion Graphics (UMG)", make sure to click the "Set as Default" button on the top of the "Editor Preferences" window, then you can close the window and go back to the main engine screen.

Before we continue, there's two more quick things we need to do:

Step #5 - Save your project as it is (Just to be safe!)

Step #6 - Close Unreal Engine 4 (Your Project and the Launcher), wait a few seconds and re-open Unreal Engine 4 (And then your project!)

NOTE: Remember to open your project in Engine version 4!

EXTRA NOTE: Don't play this one cool. I know when you install programs, some of you hit the "Restart later" button and continue to use the program like a rebel, but don't do that here because that doesn't work. You HAVE to restart the editor or Unreal Motion Graphics won't work properly!

Step #7 - Now that you've restarted your project, we need to create a new empty level. Call this new level "UMG_MainMenu" and make sure you select "Empty Level".

Save the level as it currently is and then we can begin the fun stuff!

Creating a UMG Blueprint!

Step #1 - Within the Content Browser, (Making sure you've got the "GAME" folder highlighted) create a new folder (By clicking New > Folder). Name this folder "UMG".

Step #2 - Once the folder has been created, double click "UMG" to open up the folder.

Now we're going to have some fun!

Step #3 - While still in the Content Browser (In our "UMG" folder), Right Click (Ctrl + Click) in the empty space in the folder (Which brings up the "Create" window). In this window, Scroll down to User Interface and highlight "User Interface" with your mouse, when the pop-up menu opens, select "Widget Blueprint" (Name this Blueprint "UMG_MiniTitle")

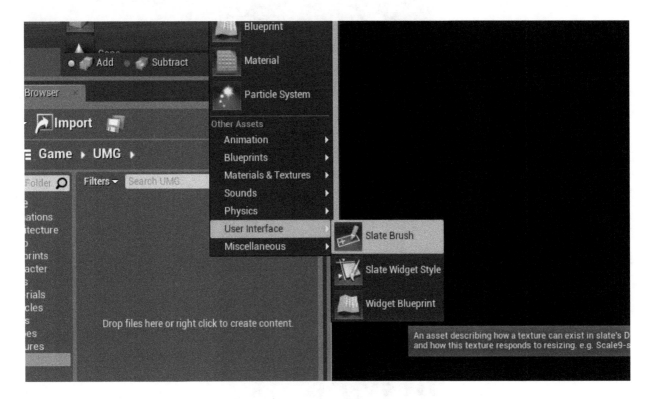

Step #4 - Double-Click the newly created "UMG_MiniTitle" to open up Unreal Motion Graphics; Now then fun REALLY begins!

Creating our Title Screen!

First things first, we're greeted with a "CanvasPanel" already placed down for us (You can see this in the bottom left under "Hierarchy". We don't need a CanvasPanel for what we're going to do, so…

Step #1 - Click on the "CanvasPanel" entry in the hierarchy and press delete on your Keyboard to do away with the useless "CanvasPanel".

Now we've got rid of the CanvasPanel, we can put in a border, which will cover our game screen edge-to-edge which will be perfect for our Main Menu background!

To create a border, we have to first find where it is hidden in UMG (Which is actually not that hidden, I mean if it were Solid Snake, it would be dead in seconds!)

Step #2 - In the "Palette" (In the top-left of the UMG window), there are a number of options just waiting to be clicked on.

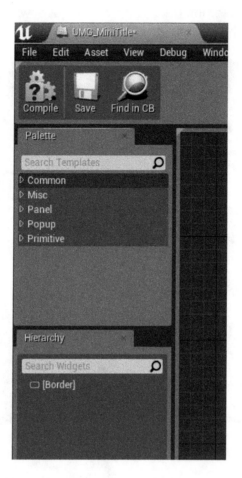

If you click on "Common", a whole new range of options are now at our disposal. To put the border into our project, all we have to do is click "Border" and drag it into the Blueprint-looking UMG view. You'll know if you've done it right as it'll now show up in the Hierarchy!

To some this wouldn't seem like doing much, but if you compare this to the HUD we created last time round, we technically created a HUD blueprint, set the resolution of the screen that the user is using and got it primed to create our HUD... In literally seconds!

Step #3 - Now our Border is ready, we can fill it with an image. To do this, we need to create a "Slate Brush". It sounds complicated but it takes a good couple of seconds.

Close out of UMG for a second and go back to the Content Browser, into your UMG folder. This is the time to import your image for the background if you haven't already (1280 x 720 image or 1920 x 1080 is ideal!)

Step #4 - Once your image has been imported, we can now create our brush. Just like you created the Widget Blueprint, do the same thing but choose Slate Widget (If you've forgotten, Right Click [Ctrl + Click] > User Interface > Slate Widget) and name this UI_Title.

Your folder should now look something like this:

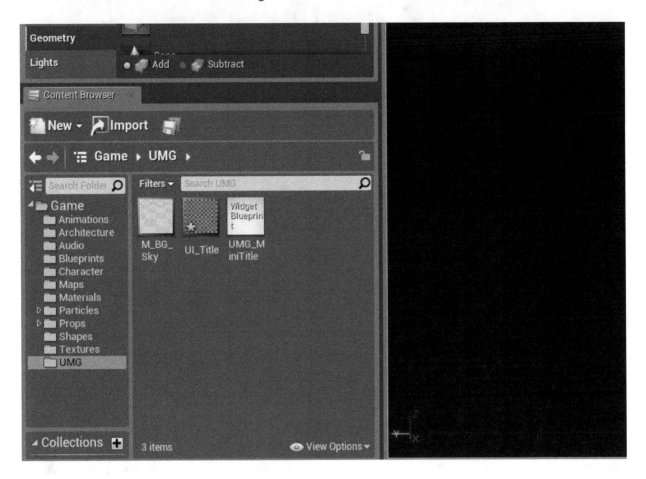

NOTE: I've already created a Material for my texture but it's down to you whether or not you want to do that.

EXTRA NOTE: Now is a good time to save!

Step #5 - Double click "UI_Title" to open up the properties, and set your "Texture or Material Asset" to your image that you have imported!

Before you move on, make sure you set the image size correctly or this will cause issues!

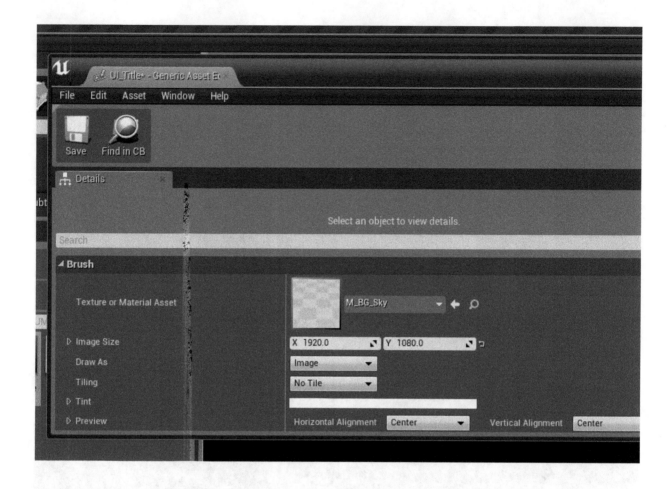

NOTE: If you're importing a Material, it might say that "This Material is not supported in UI". If this is the case, simply double click your material from within the content browser and in the properties (On the left in the Material Editor), scroll down till you see "Used with UI" and set that to true, compile, save and then all your problems that UMG is churning out should disappear!

Once you're happy with everything, save and close this window and head back into "UMG_MiniTitle"

Step #6 - Once back in UMG, Go into the Hierarchy and click "Border". This will bring up the properties on the right-hand side.

Just under "Appearance", where it says "Brush" and has a big empty white box, Simply click "None" and swap it with your Slate Brush.

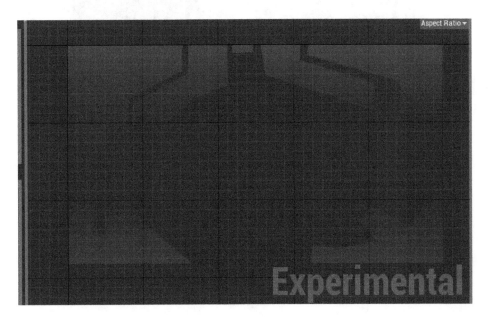

Done! Now our background image is showing, let's get making our title screen!

Buttons, Buttons, Buttons!

Now we have a background image, we need to put a button into our Title Screen so the user can navigate around, play the game, change their settings or exit your project.

To create buttons, we need to create a box that can sit on our Title Screen. To do this…

Step #1 - Head back to the Palette on the top-left and this time instead of using tools from the "Common" section, click "Panel" to bring up tools that will be extremely helpful to our cause!

This is where we need to bring the Canvas Panel back, so…
Step #2 - Simply click "Canvas Panel" and drag it into the viewport of UMG. Done.

Just to be safe, check the Hierarchy quickly to make sure the "CanvasPanel" is now sitting under the "Border" like so:

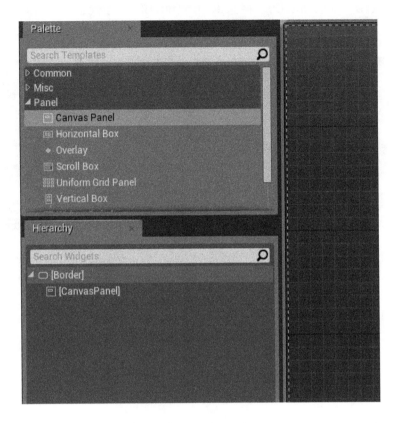

Now we can start adding buttons and whatnot to our Widget!

Step #3 - In the Hierarchy, click "CanvasPanel" to make sure what we add next goes into the CanvasPanel and not on the Border.

Once you've highlighted the CanvasPanel in the Hierachy, go back to the "Palette" box and this time click "Horizontal Box" and drag into our UMG viewport.

Step #4 - Zoom in (By using your mouse's Scroll Wheel) to the Horizontal Box and click the newly created Horizontal Box and re-size the box to cover where a long button would sit. Once you've re-sized the box, move the box near the bottom of the screen like so by clicking and dragging the box:

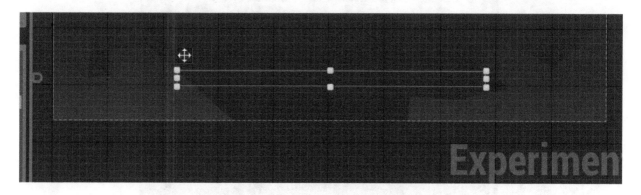

We've now created the "House" for the button, so what's next? Just before we put our button in his house to sleep, we need to tell UMG one important thing…

We need to tell UMG that no matter what the screen size, our button needs to stay in this position at the bottom of the screen. And this is how we do just that!

Step #5 - With the "Horizontal Box" still selected, go to it's options on the right of the screen and at the top under "Layout" is a section called "Anchors", it looks like this:

Step #6 - Under "Anchors" there is a grey box with the word "Anchors" written inside with a down arrow, click this down arrow and select the 10th option (Small box in the bottom centre).

This stops the button disappearing no matter what the size of the screen!

So we have the "House" all set up, it's time to put the button in it's home!

Step #7 - Head back to the "Palette" box in the left and go to the "Common" section. Within this common section, click Button and drag it INTO your Horizontal Box which you set up previously.

There's still some work left to be done before this is a fully functioning button!

The button is looking a little bare at the moment, so let's get some text inside so players find out what our button should do!

Step #8 - Just like you did with the "Button", find "Text Block" in the Palette (Which is under "Common" just like the Button was). Drag this INTO the button and you'll see just like magic the text becomes part of our button.

Step #9 - With the text selected, just like before head over to the "Details" panel on the right. This time, we need to edit the text... So just under "Content", there's a section called "Text". So can you guess what we have to do with this...? You got it!

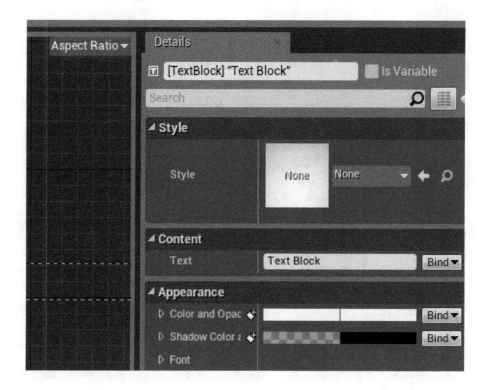

In the text box, write: "Click to Start".

I bet you're itching to know what the "Bind" button is for; But **DO NOT CLICK IT**… Just yet. We'll come back to this soon!

There's just one little thing and we're done with this button for the time being:

Step #10 - Click the "Button" (Not the text) and go into the "Details" on the right. Scroll down until you find the "Layout" section. In this section, there's a part called "Padding" and just under that is a part called "Size" with two options: "Auto" and "Fill".

Click Auto to make it fill our Horizontal Box.

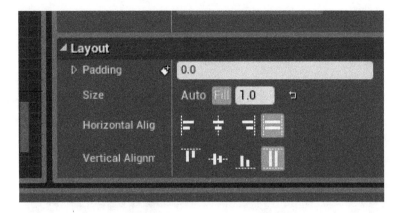

We've done what needed to be done now for this button; But it's not quite functional just yet.

Before we continue however, we need to create another Widget Blueprint, so for now:

Step #11 - "Compile" / Save and close this UMG window and in our UMG folder Right Click (Ctrl + Click) our "UMG_MiniTitle" and select "Create Copy".

Name this copy: "UMG_Title2".

Main Menu D-I-Y!

Now it's time to test your skills so I can show to you just how much you've learnt without realising it!

Your UMG folder should now look like this:

If it does, Awesome! We can continue; If not, however, then simply double-back and skim over the last chapter to check if you've missed something.

Ready to continue? Excellent!

Step #1 - Double-Click "UMG_Title2" to open up our duplicated Menu.

Step #2 - Expand all of the objects in the Hierarchy and delete the Horizontal Box, Button and Text (Deleting the Horizontal Box should delete it all for you!)

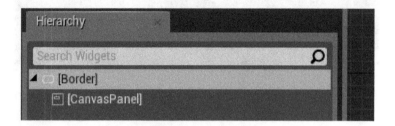

Step #3 - Now use what you've learnt so far to create this:

Remember to anchor everything to the CENTRE of the screen this time (Not the bottom) and make sure each of the buttons are in their own Horizontal Box but they're all a "Child" of the CanvasPanel.

If you need help, refresh yourself by going through the past chapter, but I believe in you and I know you can do it with no problems whatsoever!

Link to the Past

So we have a Title Screen and a Main Menu, but nothing hooking them both together. I bet you're raring to know just how to link them together; So what we are waiting for? Let's do it!

Step #1 - Save / Compile your "UMG_Title2". Once saved, close "UMG_Title2" and open "UMG_MiniTitle".

Step #2 - Click on our "Click to Start" button (Be sure to not click the text!) and head over to the details panel on the right:

Where it says "Events", there's a section called "On Clicked Event" with a "Bind" button. This means we can tell UMG what will happen when this button has been pressed, so click Bind and select "Create Binding". This will create a Blueprint for us, ready for us to mess around with.

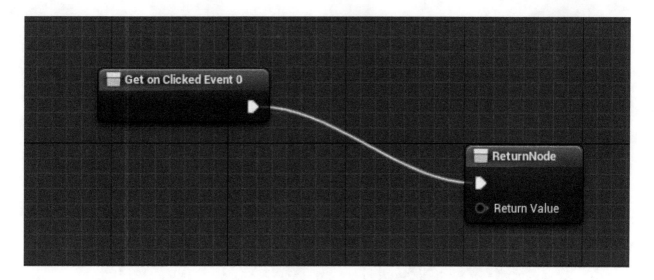

First things first, we need to break this connection as at the moment the Blueprint reads: "Start the stuff in this line > End the stuff in this line". This, obviously isn't what we want.

Step #3 - Alt+Click the arrow on the Get on Clicked Event 0 to break the connection. Now click the "Get on Click Event" node and move it a bit further to left so we have some room to play with.

Step #4 - From the empty pin on the right of "Get on Clicked Event", click and drag to the right and our favourite "Compact Blueprint Library" will open up.

Type in "Remove" and select "Remove from Viewport", this will take our current title and get rid of it.

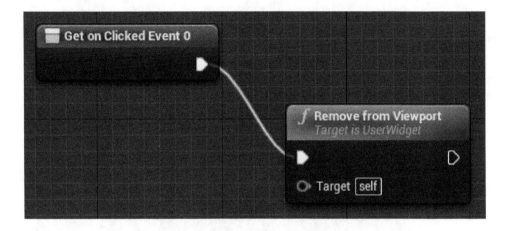

Now that we've gotten rid of the current Title Screen, we need to create the other Title Screen we created ("UMG_Title2") so it acts as a seamless transition from Title to Main Menu.

Step #5 - From the empty pin on the right of the "Remove from Viewport" node, click and drag to the right. When the CBL opens up, type in "Create Widget" and select the Create Widget node to create it.

Step #6 - Within the "Create Widget" node, there is a section called "Widget Type", with a box called "Select Class". Click "Select Class" and click "UMG_Title2_C".

This creates the second title screen, but it doesn't actually show our Title screen, it only creates it. It sounds a bit complicated, but all should make sense in a moment.

Step #7 - From the "Return Value" pin of "Create Widget", Click the blue pin and drag to the right. In the Blueprint Library, type "Add" and select "Add to Viewport".

This will bring the second title screen up, but there's a number of bools we need to tick in this node before we can use it as a Title Screen:

Modal & Show Cursor - Set these to true

Modal means the Title Screen eats up all of the inputs, so you don't accidently click behind the title screen.

Show Cursor shows the cursor.

Don't set Absolute to true as when Absolute is false means that it should take up the whole screen and not only part of it.

Step #8 - Now connect the empty right-hand side pin of "Add to Viewport" to the "Return Node" that was originally in this Blueprint and pow! That's this Blueprint done! Save and Compile the Blueprint then close UMG; It's time to tell our project to actually display these menu screens!

Let's See Our Menus!

Head into your empty level and like we've done a few times in the previous book, head into the level blueprint. If you've forgotten how to do this:

> #1 - Click the "Blueprints" button above the viewport
> #2 - Press "Open Level Blueprint

Now the Level Blueprint is open; We need to tell the Level that when the level begins, draw our menu!

As we have the first menu that draws the second menu on the button press, all we have to tell the level blueprint is to draw the first menu. So what are we waiting for?!

Step #1 - Right Click (Ctrl + Click) in empty space in the Blueprint area. When the "Compact Blueprint Library" opens up, type in "Begin" and select "Event Begin Play".

Just like before in the previous chapter, create a "Create Widget" node connected to "Event Begin Play" and then create an "Add to Viewport" node connected to the "Create Widget" node by dragging from the "Return Value" pin.

Once you've created the "Add to Viewport" node, be sure to enable the "Modal" and "Show Cursor" bools again by ticking them!

The only thing you should be doing different from before (Apart from obviously missing out the "Remove from Viewport" node!) is setting the "Widget Type" in the "Create Widget Node" to "UMG_MiniTitle_C".

NOTE: If your UMG files aren't showing up in "Widget Type" this means that one of your Widgets have had issues compiling; Usually because you forgot to connect the "Return Node" in the buttons together!

Once your level blueprint has been updated with: Event Begin Play > Create Widget > Add to Viewport as explained above, Compile the Blueprint, close the Blueprint editor and test your current project by pressing: Alt + P on your keyboard.

Congratulations! It works!

We still need to code the "New Game", "Options" and "Quit Game" buttons (Let's not get ahead of ourselves just yet! There's still one or two obstacles in our way but we'll get there in no-time!)

But this causes for a celebration; You've just created a fully working Title-Screen; So let's get the other buttons working!

Extra Buttons!

Once you've tested your menu and you're completely happy with everything; It's time to program the buttons in our "UMG_Title2" UMG Widget!

Step #1 - In the Content Browser, Open up "UMG_Title2".

Step #2 - Just like in the chapter before the chapter just gone; Create a "Bind" for all three buttons ("New Game", "Options" and "Quit Game") but don't fill out the Blueprints yet.

Once you've created "Binds" for all three buttons, go into the "Graph" tab (On the top-right) and make sure your "Functions" (In the "Variable Library" on the left) look like this:

If your "Functions" doesn't look like that, then you haven't created Binds for all three buttons; Go back until you end up with "GetOnClickEvent_0", "GetOnClickEvent_1" and "GetOnClickEvent_2" in the "Functions" area of your UMG Blueprint.

Ready to continue? Awesome!

Open up the Blueprint for "GetOnClickEvent_0" (Which should be bound to the "New Game" button).

All we have to do for this is hook up a "Open Level" node!

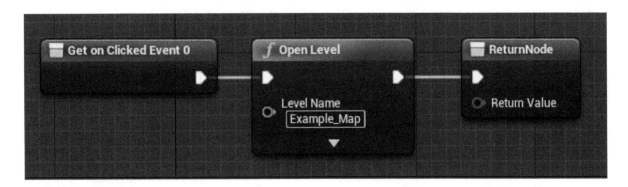

Within the "Open Level" node, there is an input called "Level Name". For demonstration purposes, let's put in "Example_Map", which will open the Example Map within our project!

What did we just do? - Basically the Blueprint reads: When the Button is clicked, open "Example_Map"! Simple... yet effective!

Compile and move over to the Blueprint "GetOnClickedEvent2" [Which should be bound to your "Quit Game" button].

I'm not talking about the "Options Button" (Which is "GetOnClickedEvent1". Do not open "GetOnClickedEvent1", open "GetOnClickedEvent2").

When you're in your "Quit Game" Blueprint ("GetOnClickedEvent2"), we need to add a "Execute Console Command" node, which is a node which (You guessed it!) executes a console command!

By now, I'm sure you can guess how to create the node, but if not, here's a hint: Right Click (Ctrl + Click). When the Compact Blueprint Library opens up, type in "Execute Console" and select the correct node!

Now, I'm sure you're wondering what "Command" needs to go into the input within "Execute Console Command", so let's not waste any time!

Within the "Command" input, simply type "Quit". Yup, that's all you have to do for this Blueprint!

So just like that, we've set up "New Game" and the "Quit Game", we're almost all done with this project! All we have to do now is couple up everything we've learnt so far as well as a few more pointers to create the "Options" menu!

These Are Your Options!

Create a new Widget Blueprint and call it "UMG_Options". Within this menu, use everything you've learned thus far to create three buttons (All with text in!), some text above these buttons and two more buttons underneath the other buttons and text. You should get something that looks like this:

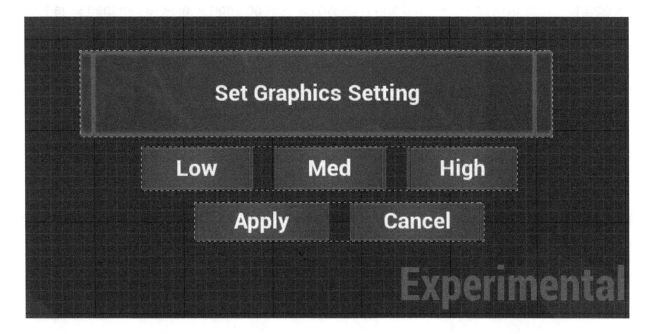

If you can't see the image, here's what you need in the relative boxes and whatnot:

- Top text box: "Set Graphics Settings"
- Three buttons under the Text Box: "Low, Med, High"
- The two buttons under the "Low, Med, High" - "Apply" and "Cancel"

Got it? Awesome! If not, Skim back through what we've already covered in the book to touch up on whatever you're missing.

Once you're ready to continue, we need to head over into the Event Graph of our "UMG_Options" (Remember to use the top ribbon to navigate!).

Just like we learnt in the last book, we need to create an Integer. Remember that? If not, here's a real quick reminder of what an Integer is and how to create one:

What is an Integer? - An Integer is a number that we can set and call back to later. Why is this important? Because we can change things if our Integer is a specific number!

"But Ryan, Why can't I use a Float? Isn't that a number we can set too?" -Well, Mystical reader who can write and be answered ala Harry Potter to Tom Riddle; A Float can deal with decimal places, which is great for storing time or anything that needs a number.number figure, but an Integer doesn't deal with decimals, It just doesn't understand them.

Instead, it prides itself on acting as a switch or a collection for WHOLE numbers only (Sorry decimal numbers, it's to the Float for you!)

"Sounds cool! But why do we need that right now?" Well, Mr / Miss / Ms / Dr, we can use an Integer to switch between Low, Med and High with almost no effort at all! We can then save that Integer and call it back WHENEVER we need it again!

"Groovitational! Let's Make One!" - Sure thing! Let's get right to it!

[NOTE: Yes, it was 5am when I wrote that, Don't mind me!]

Step #1 - If you're not there already, head into the "Graph" tab of your "UMG_Options". (Use the top-right Tab to navigate to it!)

Step #2 - On the far left, there's a window that I like to call the "Variable Library", it looks a little like this:

Step #3 - Click the "Variable" button (Which is next to Function, Macro .etc), to create a new Variable.

Step #4 - Within the details panel (Just below the "Variable Library"!), change the "Variable Type" to Int and set the name to "GraphicsSettings".

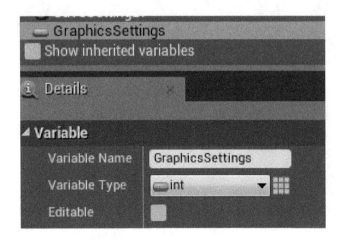

Step #5 - Done? Awesome! That's all we need to do here for the moment, so use the top-right ribbon again and go back into the "Designer" tab to go back to our UMG!

Step #6 - Click the "Low" button which you created earlier (Not the text, the button!) and in the right-hand side details panel, create a new Bind for it (Just like we did before!)

Step #7 - This will open a Blueprint editor for what happens when this button is pressed. On the left in your "Variable Library", grab your "GraphicsSettings" (You might need to scroll down in the "Variable Library" to find it!) and drag it into the Blueprint area. When asked, select "Set".

Step #8 - As this button will be the "Low" setting, keep the "GraphicsSetting" at 0 and connect both left and right white inputs to the "GetOnClickedEvent" and "ReturnNode" respectively.

Step #9 - Do exactly what we just did for both the "Med" and "High" buttons, however remember to set "GraphicsSettings" to 1 in the Mid Blueprint and 2 in the High Blueprint. Confused? Here's what you should end up with:

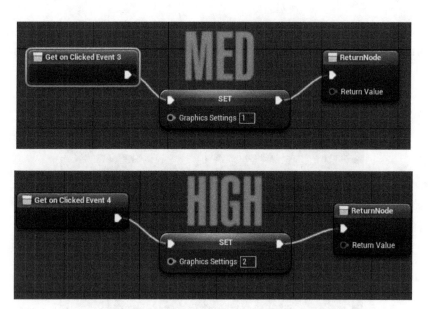

Step #10 - Three buttons down, two to go! We'll deal with Apply in two moments, but first let's take on that "Cancel" button. Create a binding for it and just like what we did from the "Title Screen" to "Options", create a "Remove for Viewport" node followed by "Create Widget" (Remember to select "UMG_Title2" in "Widget Type"!) followed by "Add to Viewport":

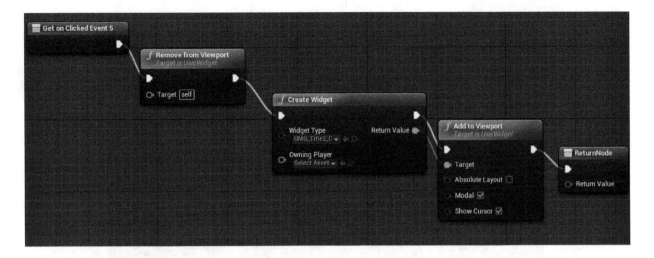

Step #11 - We've now only got one Button left to fill in; "Apply!". So what are we waiting for? Create a bind for "Apply" and let's get to coding!

Step #12 - Right Click (Ctrl+Click) to open the "Compact Blueprint Library" and type in "Switch on Int".

Step #13 - Click the "Switch On It" Node which we just created and in the "Details" panel underneath the "Variable Library", set "Default Pin" to false by unchecking the box. Once done, within the "Switch on Int" node, add two more "Pins".

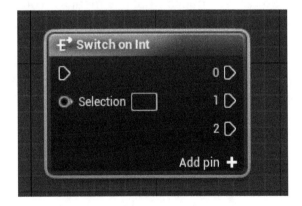

Step #14 - Doesn't that light green button next to "Selection" seem familiar? You've guessed it! Grab your "GraphicsSettings" from the "Variable Library", drag it into the Blueprint and select "Get" when asked. Hook it into Selection and connect the left input pin of the "Switch on Int" into the "GetOnClickedEvent"

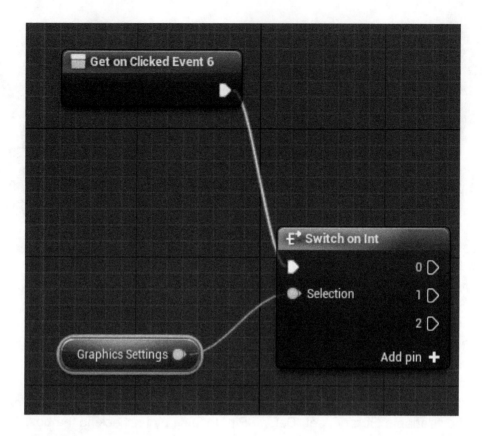

Notice that we've created three "Switch On Int" outputs: 0, 1 and 2. Just like we did with "GraphicsSettings" Integer. So can you guess what this means? You got it! 0 Stands for our "Low" option, "Med" for our Medium and "High" for our High option. But how do we change the graphics quality? Simple!

Step #15 - Right Click (Ctrl + Click) to open up the "Compact Blueprint Library" and type in "Execute Console" and select "Execute Console Command". Do this three times.

Step #16 - Hook each one of these nodes into the outputs of "Switch on Int", like so:

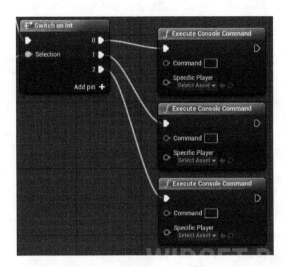

Now we need to figure out what Command to use; A quick check of the "Engine Scalability" page on the Unreal Engine site gives us a number of options to play with. For this tutorial's sake, we'll just be using "sg.PostProcessQuality".

For low, we'll use "sg.PostProcessQuality 0", Medium we'll use: "sg.PostProcessQuality 1" and for High: "sg.PostProcessQuality 3".

Step #17 - So in the "Command" area of our "Execute Console Command", in the one that stems from "Switch on Int 0" put "sg.PostProcessQuality 0". In the one stemming from "1", put "sg.PostProcessQuality 1" and "sg.PostProcessQuality 3" respectively.

So what now? I bet you're thinking we've got to do some super-complicated stuff? Nope! Simply do what we've done a few times now - Create a "Remove for Viewport" node followed by "Create Widget" (Remember to select "UMG_Title2" in "Widget Type"!) followed by "Add to Viewport".

Connect all three "Console Command" outputs to the input of "Remove from Viewport" and connect the output of "Add to Viewport" to the main output of our Blueprint like so and we're done!

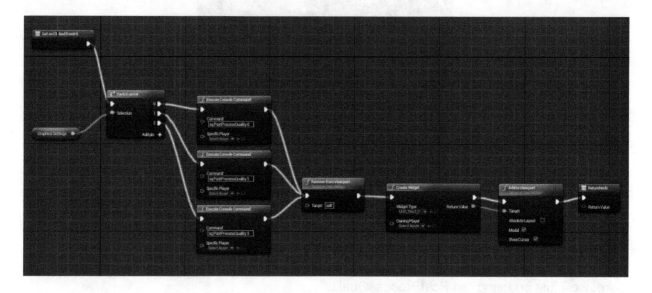

Now it's finished! We can tap ourselves on the shoulder now; We've created a working menu system! But wait… What good is this menu system if it doesn't save our preferences?

Oh-ho-ho-ho, It seems impossible but it's far more simpler then you think. But we'll save that for the next Mini-Mission! So what are you waiting for?! You made an awesome menu, now let's make it 110% more awesome!

Mission #2 - Saving & Loading

Auto-Saving & Loading our Settings!

Template:

Third-Person Blueprint

What You'll Learn:

- Saving & Loading

What You'll Need:

- The Options Menu You Created In The Last Chapter or Use The ArtOfBP_Mini#1
Project available at http://content.kitatusstudios.co.uk

Henshin A-Go-Go Baby!

Let's not dilly-dally, let's get right back into things!

Step #1 - If you're not there already, open up the Menu project we created in the last chapter; Or if you don't have that to hand, download and open the "ArtOfBP_Mini1" project files available at: http://content.kitatusstudios.co.uk

We need to create a SaveGame blueprint to store our Settings in which we've created, so head into the "UMG" folder within the Content Browser" and go to "New > Blueprint".

When it asks what type of Blueprint you'd like to create, click the "Custom Classes" button near the bottom of the Window and in the search field, type "Save" and select "SaveGame":

Step #2 - Click "Select" and name this Blueprint: "Save_SaveGraphics". Once created, double click the newly-created Blueprint to open it up. There's not a terrible amount we have to do in here; But it's crucial you don't get it wrong or none of the awesome we're about to achieve will actually work!

Step #3 - Once your Blueprint has loaded up, head over to the "Variable Library" (In the Graph tab!) and create a new Int (You remember how to, right? If not, go and skim the last chapter again!) and call it "S_Graphics".

Save & Compile this Blueprint then you can close it!

That's all we have to do for the Save blueprint!

"What?! But how does that work?!" I hear your mind scream through these pages.

Well, it's a little more complicated then what you're assuming. This Save Blueprint doesn't actually save or even load information. The Blueprint stores information that can be called at anytime. Think of it as a pocket.

A pocket doesn't have hands, so it can't give you the chocolate bar you've put in there and it can't add more chocolate bars to itself (Imagine that...) but what it does is store that Chocolate until you need it next.

So what do we have to do now? We need to create those virtual hands to feed our pocket with Chocolate bars!

Before we continue, I'd like to mention why we're about to do things the way we're about to do things - I've tried many combinations of castings and whatnot but a lot of the casting cases don't seem to work with the current Unreal Motion Graphics version in the current Unreal Engine 4 build. The way we're about to follow seems to work at the moment however!

In the main view of your Unreal Engine window (The one with the "Game View!"), There's a ribbon at the top, just above the in-game view (We covered this in Book #1!). You have a number of options in the top ribbon, such as "Quick Settings, World Settings, Blueprints, Matinee" .etc)

Step #4 - Click "World Settings", which will option a details panel in the right (Where "Details" usually are).

Step #5 - Scroll down to "GameMode" in the World Settings window, and press the "New" button. Name this GameMode Blueprint "MainMenuGameMode".

If you can't see the "Selected GameMode" options, click the Grey right arrow next to "Selected GameMode" to expand the window.

We need to create a "Player Controller", which will act as the conduit between our UMG and Save Blueprint.

Head back to our "UMG" folder and create a new Blueprint. When the "Pick Parent Class" window opens up, select Player Controller.

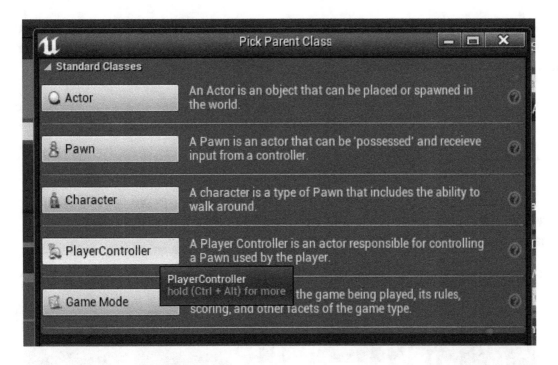

Name this Blueprint "PC_MainMenu". Now head back to the "World Settings" GameMode area and set the PlayerController to "PC_MainMenu".

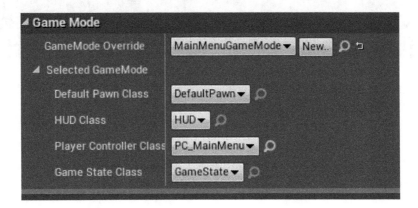

Now that it's been set, we need to configure the Blueprint itself. Double Click the "PC_MainMenu" blueprint in the Content Browser to open it up!

PlayerController = Conduit!

Step #1 - Within the "PC_MainMenu" Blueprint; Create a new Variable ("Int" again!) and call it "PC_Graphics".

Step #2 - In the Main Blueprint view, Right Click (Ctrl + Click) and create an "Event Begin Play" node.

Note: From now on, I believe you should know how to create nodes (Right Click [Ctrl + Click]) to bring up the CBL and search for the node you need. So I will no longer be telling you how to create nodes!

Step #3 - Create a "Does Save Game Exist?" node. This node does exactly what it says on the tin!

In the "SlotName" input, type in "Settings".

What is "SlotName"? When we eventually create a Save Game, this will tell the Blueprint where to look in the Save Game file! When we create the Save Game, we'll tell it to save the information into the "Settings" slot.

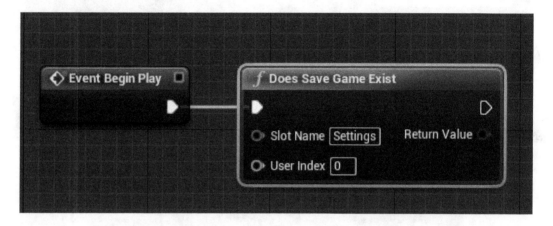

As this node poses the question: "Does Save Game Exist?", We have to give the node the ability to answer the question.

Step #4 - Create a "Branch" node (Which is essentially a "True or False" node) and hook it into the output pin of "Does Save Game Exist" and the "Condition" pin into the "Return Value" pin of "Does Save Game Exist".

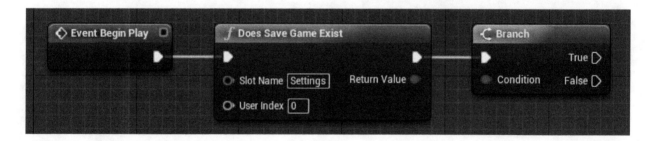

We're now going to set what happens if a "Save Game" doesn't exist. Everything we create in the next few steps will stem from the "False" output of our Branch.

SaveGame = False!

If a SaveGame doesn't exist, we're going to have to create it!

Step #1 - From the "False" output of our "Branch", create and connect a "Create Save Game Object" node.

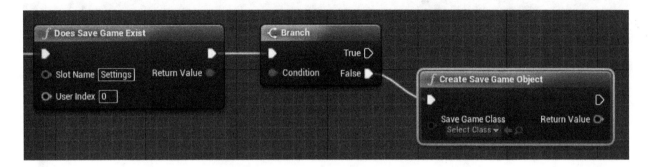

Step #2 - Within the "Create Save Game Object" node, set the "Save Game Class" under "Select Class" to "Save_SaveGraphics".

Now we need to tell the Blueprint that "SaveGraphics" is a thing and give it permission to mess around with it's variables.

Step #3 - Grab the blue pin "Return Value" and drag to the right. Type "Promote" and select "Promote to Variable".

In the Variable Window, Name this newly created Variable to "SaveGame".

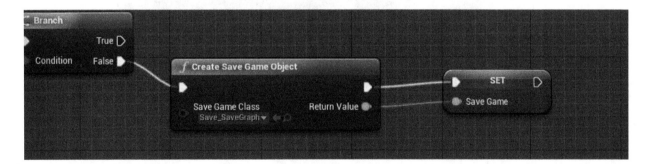

To make sure everything works alright, "Get" SaveGame from the Variable Library, put it into the Blueprint and drag from the output, typing in "Cast" (Select: Cast to Save_SaveGraphics) and connect this after the "Set SaveGame".

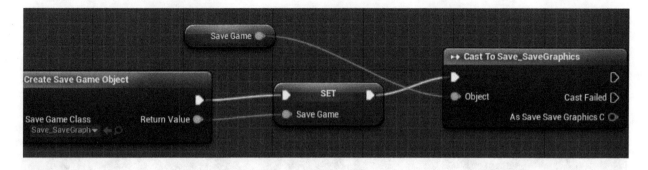

We've now created the Save Game Object, it's time to go back to the "Branch" and branch off to if the "SaveGame" is true!

SaveGame = True!

Instead of Creating a Save Game (As if the Branch is true, it already exists), we now have to "Load" the Save Game.

Step #1 - Create a "Load Game From Slot" node and connect it to the true from our "Branch".

Step #2 - Just like we did before, Set the Slot Name to "Settings" and this time drag the SaveGame variable from Variable Library and "Set" it. Hook the inputs of "Set Settings" to the right output of "Load Game From Slot" and hook the "Return Value" into "Set Settings".

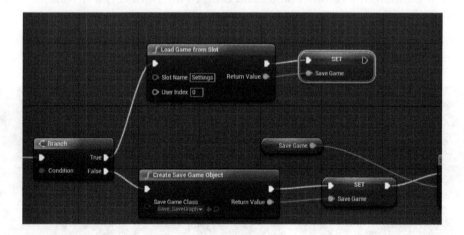

The reason we've done this is because if the Branch was false, we were setting the "SaveGame" variable. However, if the Branch is true, then obviously the Blueprint won't execute any of the "False" code.

Step #3 - Just like what we did in the "False" set of events, "Get" SaveGame and use it to "Cast to Save_SaveSettings".

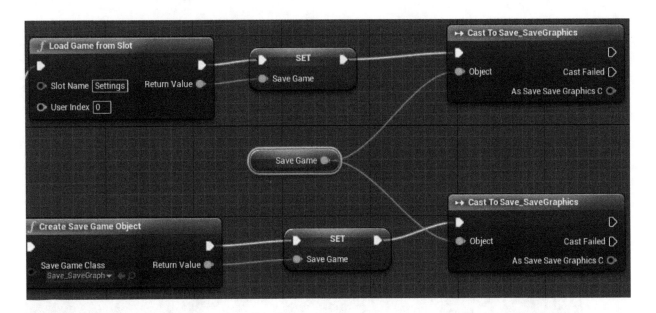

Step #4 - From the "As Save Save Graphics C", click the pin and drag to the right and type in "Get Graphics" and select it.

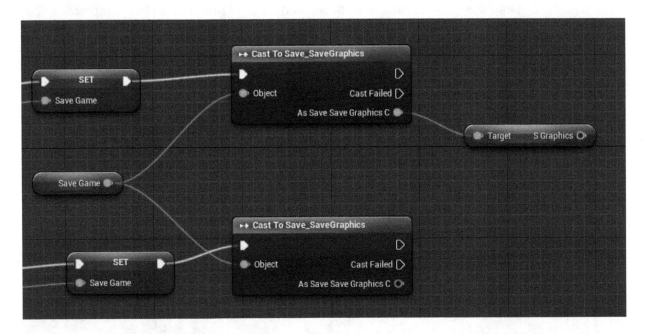

Step #5 - In the "Variable Library", drag in "PC_Graphics" and select "Set". Connect this to "Target - S_Graphics" and the top-right pin of the "Cast to Save_SaveGraphics" node.

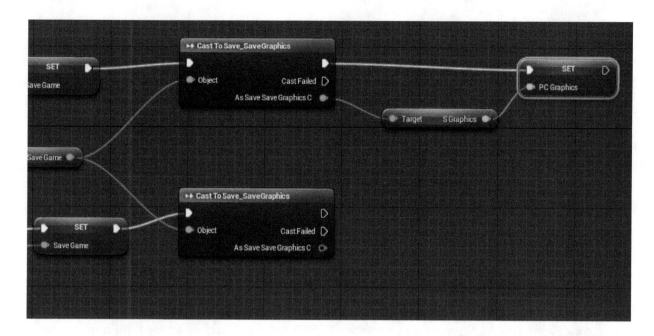

What did we just do? - We're telling the Blueprint that whatever the "Save_SaveGraphics" setting is for "S_Graphics", that is what is what we want "PC_MainMenu"'s "PC_Graphics" to be too!

It may be a tad confusing at the moment, but don't worry - Pretty soon everything will make sense!

What I want you to do now though, is to create the "Switch On Int" and "Execute Console Commands" exactly as they were back in the UMG's "Apply" button. For the Input though, use the "PC_Graphics".

You should end up with something like this:

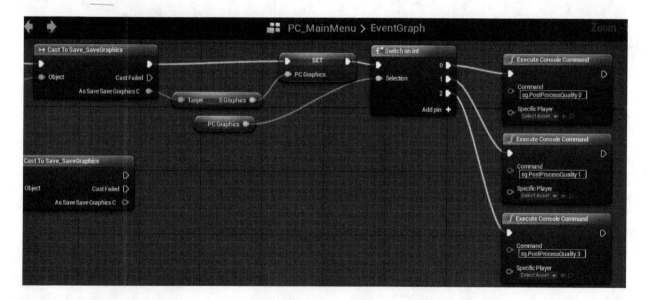

And this is the whole Blueprint for "PC_MainMenu" so far:

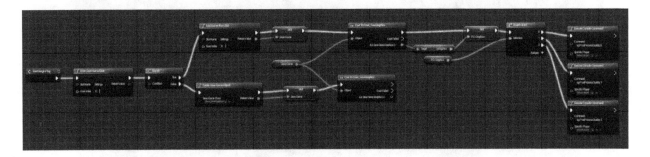

What we need to do now is set it so that when we press the "Apply" button in the UMG, it will save the changes. Here's how we're going to do that.

On Button Press, Save Our Settings!

Step #1 - While still in our "PC_MainMenu", create a new event ("Event Tick"). This means this code will fire every single frame!

Step #2 - In the "Variable Library", create a new Variable. Set it to a Bool and call it "Apply"!

Step #3 - Create a Branch, and connect it to the Tick and bring in the "Apply" bool and attach it to the Branch.

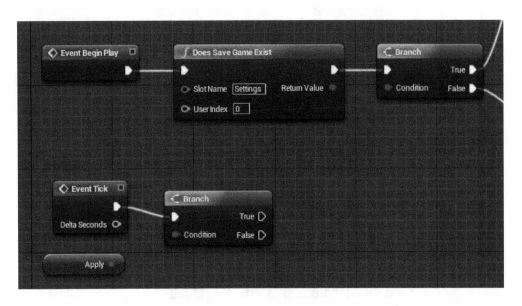

If Apply has been pressed, then we need to alter the "Save Game" file to store the new information.

Step #4 - Grab the "SaveGame" variable from the "Variable Library" and use it once again to cast to "Save_SaveGraphics" and connect this to the "True" of the Branch.

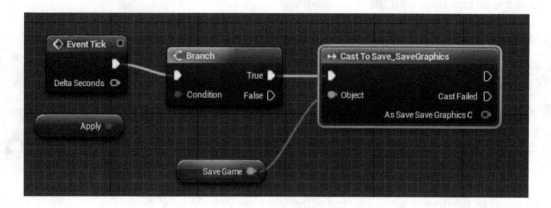

Step #5 - From the "As Save Save Graphics C", click the pin and drag to the right and type in "Set S Graphics" (Not "Get!") and select it.

Step #6 - Bring "PC_Graphics" into the Blueprint via the Variable Library once again and hook this into the "Set S Graphics" node.

Step #7 - From the right-hand side output of "Set S Graphics", create a "Save Game To Slot" node and connect them together.

Step #8 - Grab the "SaveGame" variable from the "Variable Library", drag it into the Blueprint and connect it to the "Save Game Object" and Set the SlotName to "Settings".

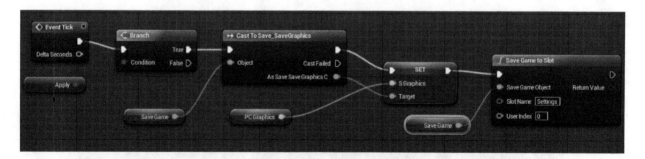

Step #9 - After "Save Game To Slot", grab "Apply" from the "Variable Library" ("Set" it when asked!) and set it to false (By leaving the checkbox unchecked)!

And we're done with this Blueprint! There's only a couple more things left to do; So what are we waiting for? Save & Compile the Blueprint then you're free to close it!

The final few steps will need an adventure back into our "MainMenuOptions" UMG Blueprint!

The Final Showdown!

Once you're back in your "MainMenuOptions", go into your "Graph" view. Open the "EventGraph" which should be in a tab above the Blueprint view. In case it's not, you can find it near the top of the Variable Library.

Step #1 - When in the EventGraph, we need an "Event Begin Play" but they don't work in UMGs. We can however use the UMG equivalent "Construct". So do just that - Create an Event Construct node.

Step #2 - Open the "Compact Blueprint Library" and type in "Get Player Controller".

Step #3 - From the "Return Value" pin of "Get Player Controller", Click and Drag to the right. When the "CBL" opens up, type in "Cast to PC_MainMenu" and connect it to the "Event Construct" node.

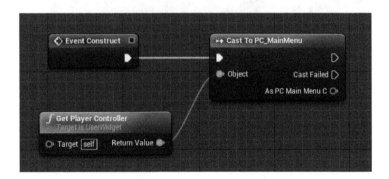

Step #4 - From "As PC Main Menu C", grab the pin and drag to the right. Type in "Get PC Graphics" and select it.

Step #5 - Go into your "Variable Library" and grab "GraphicsSettings" and drag it into the Blueprint and when asked, select "Set".

Step #6 - Connect the "Set GraphicsSettings" to the top empty output pin of the "Cast" and connect the "Get PC Graphics" output into the "Set Graphics Settings" node.

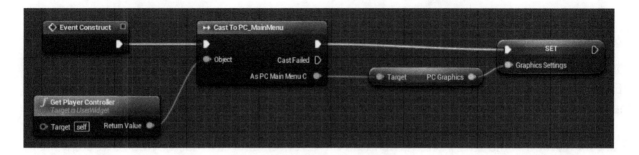

We're now so close to the finish line I can almost taste it! Save & Compile this Blueprint, then go into your "Designer" view.

Click the "Apply" button and where we created Binds before, there's a little magnifying glass next to the name of our "Bind" we created for it before. Click the magnifying glass to open it's Blueprint.

Step #1 - Alt+click the left-hand side input of "Switch On Int" to break the connection to the start of the Blueprint as we need to add a few more nodes here.

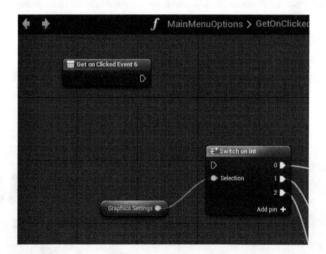

Step #2 - Just like before create the "Get Player Controller" node and use it to "Cast to PC_MainMenu".

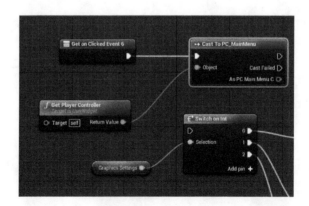

Step #3 - From "As PC Main Menu C", click and drag to the right. When the "CBL" opens up, type in "Set PC Graphics". Once the node has been created, click the pin next to "As PC Main Menu C" once again and this time type in "Set Apply".

Step #4 - In the "Set Apply" node, tick the box inside it to set "Apply" to true and connect this node into the output of "Set PC Graphics".

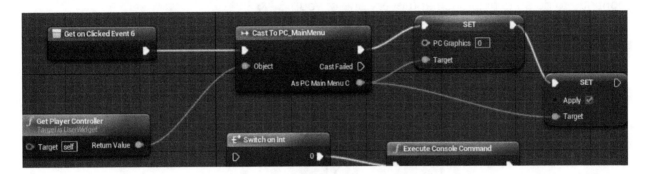

Step #5 - Head into the "Variable Library" and drag "GraphicsSettings" into the Blueprint. When asked, select "Get" and hook this into the "Set PCGraphics" node.

Now simply connect the output on the right of the "Set Apply" node and hook it into the "Switch on Int" node that we created in this Blueprint earlier.

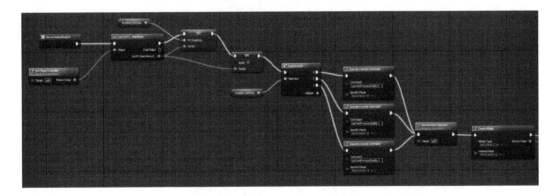

End Of The Book!

Is this the end of the book or the start of Book #3? Who knows!

In all seriousness, this has been an absolute blast! I've loved writing these books and I will continue to do so to help each and every one of you!

As always, if you've got any questions or if you'd like to show me what you've created with this book, then don't delay - email me today! - contact@kitatusstudios.co.uk

I hope you've enjoyed reading and I'll see you next time!

Peace out!
-   Ryan S, Project Lead @ Kitatus Studios.